Colorado Territorial Penitentiary, Board of Managers Reports, 1871-1877:

An Annotated Index of Marshals, Wardens, Guards, Board Members, Prisoners, and Local Businesses

Indexed by Dina C. Carson

Colorado Territorial Penitentiary, Board of Managers Reports, 1871-1877:

An Annotated Index of Marshals, Wardens, Guards, Board Members, Prisoners, and Local Businesses

Indexed by Dina C. Carson

Published by:

Iron Gate Publishing
P.O. Box 999
Niwot, CO 80544
www.irongate.com

All rights reserved. No part of this book may be reproduced or transmitted in any form or by any means, electronic or mechanical, including photocopying, recording or any information storage and retrieval system without written permission from the author, except for the inclusion of brief quotations in a review.

The Publisher of this directory makes no representation that it is absolutely accurate or complete. Errors and omissions, whether typographical, clerical or otherwise do sometimes occur and may occur anywhere within the body of this publication. The Publisher does not assume and hereby disclaims any liability to any party for loss or damage by errors or omissions in this publication, whether such errors or omissions result from negligence, accident or any other cause.

Iron Gate Publishing has used its best efforts in collecting and preparing material for inclusion in *Colorado Territorial Penitentiary, Board of Managers Reports, 1871-1877: An Annotated Index of Marshals, Wardens, Guards, Board Members, Prisoners, and Local Businesses*, but does not warrant that the information herein is complete or accurate, and does not assume, and hereby disclaims, any liability to any person for any loss or damage caused by errors or omissions in *Colorado Territorial Penitentiary, Board of Managers Reports, 1871-1877: An Annotated Index of Marshals, Wardens, Guards, Board Members, Prisoners, and Local Businesses*, whether such errors or omissions result from negligence, accident or any other cause.

Copyright © 2019 by Dina C. Carson, Iron Gate Publishing

Printed in the United States of America

ISBN 1-68224-039-8   ISBN 13 978-1-68224-039-7

Introduction

The *Colorado Territorial Penitentiary, Board of Managers Reports, 1871-1877: An Annotated Index of Marshals, Wardens, Guards, Board Members, Prisoners, and Local Businesses* contains the names of the penitentiary's first one hundred prisoners (including escapees), a physical description of the person, why they were in the penitentiary, which county sentenced them and where they were born.

In addition, the Board of Managers Reports included the services provided to the prison by local businesses, the names of each member of the Board, along with the names of US Marshals, wardens, guards, nurses and other personnel.

An inventory dated 1 Dec 1874 shows a prison (40'x70'), a guard's sleeping apartment, a guard's dining room and prison kitchen, the warden's residence (brick, 6 rooms and hall, one outhouse and store house), a shoemaker's shop (adobe with cellar), a carpenter's show (wood 15'x20'), a blacksmith's shop (wood 14'x17'), a stone cutter's shop (wood, 15'x32'), two outhouses for general use, a bake oven (10'x12'), 360' of stone embankment in front of the prison, 330' of picket fence with 2 single gates and 1 double gate, 700' of board fence around the garden, all on 40 acres of land.

The original files that make up the *Colorado Territorial Penitentiary, Board of Managers Reports, 1871-1877: An Annotated Index of Marshals, Wardens, Guards, Board Members, Prisoners, and Local Businesses* are held by the Colorado State Archives and are accessible for research. You can order a copies of these documents by calling the Colorado State Archives, or placing an order through their website.

A

Abner, Louis
- 1874 Dec 1, FF3, Convicts in Colorado Penitentiary on 1 Dec 1874, prisoner, Crime: burglary, County: Arapahoe, Sentence: 3 yr., Age: 22, laborer, 5' 5 1/2"
- 1874 Dec 23, FF3, Convicts received at the Colorado State Penitentiary from 13 June 1871 to 1 Dec 1874, Prisoner no. 98, Crime: burglary, County: Arapahoe, Sentence: 3 yr, Age: 22, Occupation: laborer, 5 ' 5 1/2", Complexion: colored, Hair: black, Eyes: black, Nativity: TN, Education: reads and writes

Adams & Locke
- 1874 Nov, FF3, Expenditures and Earnings of the Colorado Penitentiary, stone

Agard, A G
- 1876 Dec 31, FF4, Report of the Treasurer, vendor

Agard, A Y
- 1876 Feb 17, FF4, Balance sheet, vendor
- 1876 Apr 7, FF4, Balance sheet, vendor
- 1876 July 10, FF4, Balance sheet, vendor
- 1877 Apr 11, FF4, Balance sheet, vendor

Agard, J C
- 1877 Apr 11, FF4, Balance sheet, vendor

Agard, N R
- 1877 Apr 11, FF4, Balance sheet, vendor

Agard, W R
- 1875 Aug 31, FF4, Balance Sheet, vendor
- 1875 Sept 1, FF4, Schedule of Vouchers Drawn, Guard
- 1876 Dec 31, FF4, Report of the Treasurer, vendor
- 1876 July 10, FF4, Balance sheet, vendor
- 1876 Oct 13, FF4, Balance sheet, vendor
- 1877 Jan 1, FF4, Balance sheet, vendor

Alberton, Ed
- 1871 Dec, FF4, December Bill for Fees, prisoner
- 1871 Nov, FF4, November Bill for Fees, prisoner
- 1871 Oct, FF4, October Bill for Fees, prisoner
- 1871 Oct 1, FF4, September Bill for Fees, prisoner

Albretton, Ed
- 1872, Aug 31, FF4, Aug Bill for Fees, prisoner
- 1873 Aug 31, FF4, Aug Bill for Fees, prisoner
- 1873 July 31, FF4, July Bill for Fees, prisoner
- 1873 June 30, FF4, June Bill for Fees, prisoner

Albritton, Ed
- 1871 July 9, FF3, Convicts dismissed from Colorado Penitentiary 13 June 1871 to 1 Dec 1874, prisoner, release no. 6, Crime: larceny, County: Arapahoe, Sentence: 3 yr, Age: 21, discharged 1874 Mar 2, pardoned by Gov Elbert
- 1872 Apr, FF4, April Bill for Fees, prisoner
- 1872 Jan, FF4, January Bill for Fees, prisoner
- 1872 July, FF4, July Bill for Fees, prisoner
- 1872 May, FF4, May Bill for Fees, prisoner

Albritton, Edward
- 1874 Dec 23, FF3, Convicts received at the Colorado State Penitentiary from 13 June 1871 to 1 Dec 1874, Prisoner no. 6, Crime: larceny, County: Arapahoe, Sentence: 1 yr, Age: 21, Occupation: laborer, 5 ' 7 1/4", Complexion: colored, Hair: black, Eyes: black, Nativity: OH, Education: reads and writes

Albutton, Edward
- 1872 Dec 31, FF4, Dec Bill for Fees, prisoner
- 1873 Apr 30, FF4, April Bill for Fees, prisoner
- 1873 May 31, FF4, May Bill for Fees, prisoner

Allen & Meckheiser
- 1874 Dec 1, FF4, Minutes of the Board of Managers, hardware

Allen & Werkheiser
- 1874 Aug, FF3, Expenditures and

Colorado Territorial Penitentiary

Earnings of the Colorado Penitentiary, hardware
1874 Aug 31, FF4, Minutes of the Board of Managers, vendor
1874 June, FF3, Cash Accounts from the Books of A Rudd
1874 May, FF3, Cash Accounts from the Books of A Rudd
1874 May, FF3, Convict Labor Administered by Anson Rudd, 2 1/2 days
1874 May 29, FF4, Statement of Accounts, hardware
1874 Nov, FF3, Expenditures and Earnings of the Colorado Penitentiary, hardware
1874 Sept 15, FF3, Cash Accounts of the Colorado Penitentiary

Allen, B F
1874 May, FF3, Convict Labor Administered by Anson Rudd, 12 days
1876 Apr 1, FF4, Balance sheet, vendor
1876 Dec 31, FF4, Report of the Treasurer, vendor

Allen, Benj F
1876 Jan 1, FF4, Balance sheet, vendor

Allen, Capt B F
1875 Dec 7, FF4, Minutes of the Board of Managers, Warden (appointed)

Alling & Co
1876 Apr 7, FF4, Balance sheet, vendor
1876 Dec 31, FF4, Report of the Treasurer, vendor
1876 July 10, FF4, Balance sheet, vendor
1876 Oct 13, FF4, Balance sheet, vendor
1877 Apr 11, FF4, Balance sheet, vendor
1877 Jan 1, FF4, Balance sheet, vendor

Alling Curtis & Co
1876 Feb 17, FF4, Balance sheet, vendor

Alling, Curtice & Co
1876 Dec 31, FF4, Report of the Treasurer, vendor

American House
1875 June 4, FF4, Minutes of the Board of Managers, meeting place in Denver

Apodaca, Antonio
1872 Dec 31, FF4, Dec Bill for Fees, prisoner
1872 July 14, FF3, Convicts dismissed from Colorado Penitentiary 13 June 1871 to 1 Dec 1874, prisoner, release no. 39, Crime: larceny, County: Las Animas, Sentence: 2 yr, Age: 38, discharged 1874 June 20, no remarks
1872, Aug 31, FF4, Aug Bill for Fees, prisoner
1873 Apr 30, FF4, April Bill for Fees, prisoner
1873 Aug 31, FF4, Aug Bill for Fees, prisoner
1873 July 31, FF4, July Bill for Fees, prisoner
1873 June 30, FF4, June Bill for Fees, prisoner
1873 May 31, FF4, May Bill for Fees, prisoner
1874 Dec 23, FF3, Convicts received at the Colorado State Penitentiary from 13 June 1871 to 1 Dec 1874, Prisoner no. 48, Crime: larceny, County: Las Animas, Sentence: 2 yr, Age: 38, Occupation: laborer, 5 ' 10", Complexion: dark, Hair: black, Eyes: hazel, Nativity: NM, Education: none

Appleyard, G
1874 July 24, FF3, Cash Accounts of the Colorado Penitentiary

Appleyard, G A
1874 Dec 31, FF4, Expenses paid for G W Graham & Switterline, US Prisoners, nurse at Rosita
1875 Jan 1, FF4, Bill for G W Graham, nurse at Rosita

Austin, I A
1876 Oct 13, FF4, Balance sheet, vendor
1877 Jan 1, FF4, Balance sheet, vendor

Austin, J A
1877 Apr 11, FF4, Balance sheet, vendor

Austin, Jos H
1876 Dec 31, FF4, Report of the Treasurer, vendor

Board of Managers Reports, 1871-1877

Austin, Joseph
 1876 Dec 31, FF4, Report of the Treasurer, vendor
 1876 July 10, FF4, Balance sheet, vendor

Austin, Joseph A
 1876 Dec 31, FF4, Report of the Treasurer, vendor

Avalanche, The
 1876 Oct 13, FF4, Balance sheet, vendor

Avery, A
 1874 Dec 1, FF4, Balance sheet, vendor
 1874 June, FF3, Expenditures and Earnings of the Colorado Penitentiary, gloves, shirt
 1875 Aug 31, FF4, Balance Sheet, vendor
 1875 Dec 6, FF4, Schedule of Open Accounts, vendor

B

Baer, J C
 1874 Dec 1, FF4, Balance sheet, vendor
 1874 May, FF3, Convict Labor Administered by Anson Rudd, 15 days

Bailey, R B
 1875 Mar 1, FF4, Minutes of the Board of Managers, Guard

Bain & McGrew
 1876 Dec 31, FF4, Report of the Treasurer, vendor
 1876 July 10, FF4, Balance sheet, vendor
 1876 Oct 13, FF4, Balance sheet, vendor
 1877 Jan 1, FF4, Balance sheet, vendor

Bain & Reynolds
 1874 Nov, FF3, Expenditures and Earnings of the Colorado Penitentiary, convict labor
 1874 Nov 13, FF3, Cash Accounts of the Colorado Penitentiary
 1874 Oct, FF3, Expenditures and Earnings of the Colorado Penitentiary, setting pier

Baker, H
 1876 Oct 13, FF4, Balance sheet, vendor

Baker, Harry
 1876 Dec 31, FF4, Report of the Treasurer, vendor
 1876 July 10, FF4, Balance sheet, vendor

Baker, M F
 1875 Dec 7, FF4, Minutes of the Board of Managers, vendor

Baker, N F
 1875 Dec 6, FF4, Schedule of Vouchers Drawn, vendor

Baker, W F
 1876 Apr 7, FF4, Balance sheet, vendor
 1876 Dec 31, FF4, Report of the Treasurer, vendor
 1876 July 10, FF4, Balance sheet, vendor
 1876 Oct 13, FF4, Balance sheet, vendor
 1877 Apr 11, FF4, Balance sheet, vendor

Baker, W F
 1877 Jan 1, FF4, Balance sheet, vendor

Baker, Wm F
 1876 Feb 17, FF4, Balance sheet, vendor

Baldwin, W F
 1875 Aug 31, FF4, Balance Sheet, vendor
 1875 Dec 6, FF4, Schedule of Vouchers Drawn, vendor
 1875 Dec 7, FF4, Minutes of the Board of Managers, vendor

Baldwin, W H
 1875 Sept 2, FF4, Minutes of the Board of Managers, Clerk & Turnkey

Ballman, Thomas
 1875 Aug 31, FF4, Balance Sheet, vendor

Ballman, Thos
 1875 Dec 6, FF4, Schedule of Vouchers Drawn, vendor

Ballman, Wm
 1875 Dec 6, FF4, Schedule of Vouchers Drawn, vendor
 1876 Apr 7, FF4, Balance sheet, vendor
 1876 Dec 31, FF4, Report of the Treasurer, vendor
 1876 July 10, FF4, Balance sheet, vendor
 1876 Oct 13, FF4, Balance sheet, vendor
 1877 Apr 11, FF4, Balance sheet, vendor
 1877 Jan 1, FF4, Balance sheet, vendor

Colorado Territorial Penitentiary

Balman, Wm
   1875 Dec 7, FF4, Minutes of the Board of Managers, vendor
   1876 Dec 31, FF4, Report of the Treasurer, vendor

Barlow (Cook, Chandler & Barlow)
   1874 Dec 1, FF4, Balance sheet, vendor
   1874 Dec 1, FF4, Minutes of the Board of Managers, cloth
   1874 Nov, FF3, Expenditures and Earnings of the Colorado Penitentiary, cloth
   1874 Oct, FF3, Expenditures and Earnings of the Colorado Penitentiary, cloth
   1875 Mar 1, FF4, Minutes of the Board of Managers, cloth
   1875 Mar 1, FF4, Minutes of the Board of Managers, cloth
   1876 Apr 7, FF4, Balance sheet, vendor
   1876 Dec 31, FF4, Report of the Treasurer, vendor
   1876 Feb 17, FF4, Balance sheet, vendor
   1876 Oct 13, FF4, Balance sheet, vendor

Barlow, Sanderson & Co Road
   1874 May, FF3, Convict Labor Administered by Anson Rudd, 38 days

Barrett, T E
   1875 Jan 1, FF4, Bill for G W Graham, nurse at Rosita

Barrett, Thomas E
   1874 Dec 31, FF4, Expenses paid for G W Graham & Switterline, US Prisoners, nurse at Rosita

Barrette, T E
   1874 July 7, FF3, Cash Accounts of the Colorado Penitentiary

Bartholomew, William
   1872 Apr, FF4, April Bill for Fees, prisoner
   1872 Dec 31, FF4, Dec Bill for Fees, prisoner
   1872 July, FF4, July Bill for Fees, prisoner
   1872 May, FF4, May Bill for Fees, prisoner
   1872, Aug 31, FF4, Aug Bill for Fees, prisoner

Bartholomew, Wm
   1872 Feb 7, FF3, Convicts dismissed from Colorado Penitentiary 13 June 1871 to 1 Dec 1874, prisoner, release no. 27, Crime: burglary, County: Arapahoe, Sentence: 1 yr, Age: 27, discharged 1872 Dec 22, no remarks
   1874 Dec 23, FF3, Convicts received at the Colorado State Penitentiary from 13 June 1871 to 1 Dec 1874, Prisoner no. 33, Crime: burglary, County: Arapahoe, Sentence: 1 yr, Age: 27, Occupation: carpenter, 5 ' 5", Complexion: dark, Hair: dk brown, Eyes: lt brown, Nativity: England, Education: reads and writes

Bartlett, E G W
   1877 Apr 11, FF4, Balance sheet, vendor
   1877 Jan 1, FF4, Balance sheet, vendor

Baxter, O H P
   1876 Dec 31, FF4, Report of the Treasurer, vendor

Beals, Moses
   1874 Dec 23, FF3, Convicts received at the Colorado State Penitentiary from 13 June 1871 to 1 Dec 1874, Prisoner no. 77, Crime: burglary, County: Arapahoe, Sentence: 1 yr, Age: 21, Occupation: hostler, 5 ' 6", Complexion: light, Hair: dark, Eyes: grey, Nativity: KY, Education: reads only
   1874 Mar 18, FF3, Convicts dismissed from Colorado Penitentiary 13 June 1871 to 1 Dec 1874, prisoner, release no. 56, Crime: burglary, County: Arapahoe, Sentence: 1 yr, Age: 21, discharged 1874 Oct 3, pardoned by Act Gov Jenkins

Bell, Chas A
   1874 Dec 1, FF3, Convicts in Colorado Penitentiary on 1 Dec 1874, prisoner, Crime: burglary, County: Jefferson, Sentence: 1 yr, Age: 31, Occupation: laborer, 5 ' 9 3/4"
   1874 Dec 1, FF3, Convicts in Colorado Penitentiary on 1 Dec 1874, prisoner, Crime: burglary, County: Arapahoe, Sentence: 2 yr, Age: 30, Occupation: cabinet maker, 5 ' 7"

1874 Dec 23, FF3, Convicts received at the Colorado State Penitentiary from 13 June 1871 to 1 Dec 1874, Prisoner no. 89, Crime: burglary, County: Arapahoe, Sentence: 2 yt, Age: 30, Occupation: cabinet maker, 5 ' 7", Complexion: medium, Hair: dark, Eyes: hazel, Nativity: PA, Education: reads and writes

1874 Dec 23, FF3, Convicts received at the Colorado State Penitentiary from 13 June 1871 to 1 Dec 1874, Prisoner no. 100, Crime: burglary, County: Jefferson, Sentence: 1 yr, Age: 31, Occupation: laborer, 5 ' 9 3/4", Complexion: fair, Hair: dark, Eyes: blue, Nativity: NY, Education: reads and writes

Bennett, Charles C
1871 Dec, FF4, December Bill for Fees, prisoner
1871 Nov, FF4, November Bill for Fees, prisoner
1872 Apr, FF4, April Bill for Fees, prisoner
1872 Dec 31, FF4, Dec Bill for Fees, prisoner
1872 Jan, FF4, January Bill for Fees, prisoner
1872 July, FF4, July Bill for Fees, prisoner
1872 May, FF4, May Bill for Fees, prisoner
1872, Aug 31, FF4, Aug Bill for Fees, prisoner
1873 Apr 30, FF4, April Bill for Fees, prisoner
1873 Aug 31, FF4, Aug Bill for Fees, prisoner
1873 July 31, FF4, July Bill for Fees, prisoner
1873 June 30, FF4, June Bill for Fees, prisoner
1873 May 31, FF4, May Bill for Fees, prisoner

Bennett, Chas C
1874 Dec 1, FF3, Convicts in Colorado Penitentiary on 1 Dec 1874, prisoner, Crime: murder, County: Arapahoe, Sentence: life, Age: 21, Occupation: teamster, 5 ' 6"

1874 Dec 23, FF3, Convicts received at the Colorado State Penitentiary from 13 June 1871 to 1 Dec 1874, Prisoner no. 22, Crime: murder, County: Arapahoe, Sentence: life, Age: 21, Occupation: teamster, 5 ' 6", Complexion: florid, Hair: dk brown, Eyes: brown, Nativity: MO, Education: reads and writes

Bertenshaw, L
1877 Jan 1, FF4, Balance sheet, vendor

Bertenshow, Silas
1876 Dec 31, FF4, Report of the Treasurer, vendor

Bolman, William
1876 Dec 31, FF4, Report of the Treasurer, vendor

Born, Gus W
1873 Apr 30, FF4, April Bill for Fees, prisoner
1873 Aug 31, FF4, Aug Bill for Fees, prisoner
1873 Jan 1, FF3, Convicts dismissed from Colorado Penitentiary 13 June 1871 to 1 Dec 1874, prisoner, release no. 44, Crime: larceny, County: Arapahoe, Sentence: 2 yr, Age: 34, discharged 1874 Apr 14, pardoned by Act Gov Jenkins
1873 July 31, FF4, July Bill for Fees, prisoner
1873 June 30, FF4, June Bill for Fees, prisoner
1873 May 31, FF4, May Bill for Fees, prisoner
1874 Dec 23, FF3, Convicts received at the Colorado State Penitentiary from 13 June 1871 to 1 Dec 1874, Prisoner no. 53, Crime: larceny, County: Arapahoe, Sentence: 2 yr, Age: 34, Occupation: carpenter, 5 ' 5 1/2", Complexion: dark, Hair: black, Eyes: grey, Nativity: Russia, Education: reads and writes

Boyd, Joseph T
1874 Aug 31, FF4, Minutes of the Board of Managers, Board Member
1874 Dec 1, FF4, Minutes of the Board of Managers, Board Member

Colorado Territorial Penitentiary

1874 Dec 23, FF3, Convicts received at the Colorado State Penitentiary from 13 June 1871 to 1 Dec 1874, Board of Penitentiary Managers

1874 Dec 23, FF3, warden's letter, Board of Penitentiary Managers

1875 Mar 1, FF4, Minutes of the Board of Managers, Board Member

1875 Mar 3, FF4, Minutes of the Board of Managers, Board Member

1875 Sept 2, FF4, Minutes of the Board of Managers, Board Member

Boyd, Mr

1875 Dec 7, FF4, Minutes of the Board of Managers, Board Member

1875 June 1, FF4, Minutes of the Board of Managers, Board Member

1875 June 4, FF4, Minutes of the Board of Managers, Board Member

Bradbury, Dr

1874 Dec 31, FF4, Expenses paid for G W Graham & Switterline, US Prisoners, Doctor at Rosita

Bradbury, J M

1874 Aug 18, FF3, Cash Accounts of the Colorado Penitentiary

Brandegee, T S

1874 Dec 1, FF4, Minutes of the Board of Managers, Svereging

Brandegru, T S

1874 Nov, FF3, Expenditures and Earnings of the Colorado Penitentiary, surveying

Braundise, F S

1874 May 29, FF4, Statement of Accounts, surveying

Brewster, O S

1874 Dec 1, FF4, Minutes of the Board of Managers, milk

1874 July, FF3, Expenditures and Earnings of the Colorado Penitentiary, milk

1874 July 24, FF3, Cash Accounts of the Colorado Penitentiary

1874 Nov, FF3, Expenditures and Earnings of the Colorado Penitentiary, milk

1874 Nov 3, FF3, Cash Accounts of the Colorado Penitentiary

1874 Oct, FF3, Expenditures and Earnings of the Colorado Penitentiary, milk

1875 Dec 6, FF4, Schedule of Vouchers Drawn, vendor

1875 Dec 7, FF4, Minutes of the Board of Managers, vendor

Brown & Bros

1876 Apr 7, FF4, Balance sheet, vendor

Brown Bros

1874 Aug 31, FF4, Minutes of the Board of Managers, vendor

1874 May, FF3, Cash Accounts from the Books of A Rudd

1874 May, FF3, Cash Accounts from the Books of A Rudd

1874 Sept, FF3, Expenditures and Earnings of the Colorado Penitentiary, drayage

1874 Sept 14, FF3, Cash Accounts of the Colorado Penitentiary

1876 Dec 31, FF4, Report of the Treasurer, vendor

Brown, Charles

1873 Apr 30, FF4, April Bill for Fees, prisoner

1873 Aug 31, FF4, Aug Bill for Fees, prisoner

1873 July 31, FF4, July Bill for Fees, prisoner

1873 June 30, FF4, June Bill for Fees, prisoner

1873 May 31, FF4, May Bill for Fees, prisoner

Brown, Chas

1873 Jan 25, FF3, Convicts dismissed from Colorado Penitentiary 13 June 1871 to 1 Dec 1874, prisoner, release no. 49, Crime: murder, County: El Paso, Sentence: 3 yr, Age: 32, discharged 1874 Nov 10, pardoned by Gov McCook

1874 Dec 23, FF3, Convicts received at the Colorado State Penitentiary from 13 June 1871 to 1 Dec 1874, Prisoner no. 58, Crime: murder, County: El Paso, Sentence: 3 yr, Age: 32, Occupation: farmer, 5 ' 9 1/4", Complexion: florid, Hair: auburn, Eyes: grey, Nativity: Canada, Education: reads and writes

Brown, Herman
1874 Dec 23, FF3, Convicts received at the Colorado State Penitentiary from 13 June 1871 to 1 Dec 1874, Prisoner no. 79, Crime: larceny, County: Pueblo, Sentence: 2 yr, Age: 32, Occupation: cook, 5 ' 7", Complexion: dark, Hair: dark, Eyes: brown, Nativity: Ireland, Education: reads only

Brunn Bros
1874 May 29, FF4, Statement of Accounts, coal and wood

Buckley, John
1875 Dec 6, FF4, Schedule of Vouchers Drawn, vendor
1875 Dec 6, FF4, Schedule of Vouchers Drawn, vendor
1875 Dec 7, FF4, Minutes of the Board of Managers, vendor
1876 Apr 7, FF4, Balance sheet, vendor
1876 Dec 31, FF4, Report of the Treasurer, vendor
1876 Feb 17, FF4, Balance sheet, vendor

Burdett, E G W
1876 Dec 31, FF4, Report of the Treasurer, vendor

Burdett, G W
1876 Dec 31, FF4, Report of the Treasurer, vendor
1876 Oct 13, FF4, Balance sheet, vendor
1877 Apr 11, FF4, Balance sheet, vendor

Burdett, Geo W
1876 Apr 7, FF4, Balance sheet, vendor
1876 July 10, FF4, Balance sheet, vendor

Burdett, Wm
1874 June, FF3, Cash Accounts from the Books of A Rudd

Burdett, Y W
1877 Jan 1, FF4, Balance sheet, vendor

Burke, John
1876 Apr 7, FF4, Balance sheet, vendor
1876 Dec 31, FF4, Report of the Treasurer, vendor

Butler, Henry
1876 Oct 13, FF4, Balance sheet, vendor

Butter, Henry
1876 Dec 31, FF4, Report of the Treasurer, vendor

Buttolph, Cassius
1873 Apr 30, FF4, April Bill for Fees, prisoner
1873 Aug 31, FF4, Aug Bill for Fees, prisoner
1873 July 31, FF4, July Bill for Fees, prisoner
1873 June 30, FF4, June Bill for Fees, prisoner
1873 May 31, FF4, May Bill for Fees, prisoner

Buttolph, Cassius H
1872 Dec 10, FF3, Convicts dismissed from Colorado Penitentiary 13 June 1871 to 1 Dec 1874, prisoner, release no. 40, Crime: larceny, County: Weld, Sentence: 3 yr, Age: 22, discharged 1873 Sept 27, pardoned by Gov Elbert
1874 Dec 23, FF3, Convicts received at the Colorado State Penitentiary from 13 June 1871 to 1 Dec 1874, Prisoner no. 49, Crime: larceny, County: Weld, Sentence: 3 yr, Age: 22, Occupation: laborer, 5 ' 8", Complexion: light, Hair: light, Eyes: blue, Nativity: PA, Education: reads and writes

Byers, W N
1876 Dec 31, FF4, Report of the Treasurer, vendor

Byers, Wm N
1876 Apr 7, FF4, Balance sheet, vendor

C

Callison, John
1875 Dec 6, FF4, Schedule of Vouchers Drawn, vendor
1875 Dec 6, FF4, Schedule of Vouchers Drawn, vendor
1875 Dec 7, FF4, Minutes of the Board of Managers, vendor
1875 June 4, FF4, Minutes of the Board of Managers, vendor

Colorado Territorial Penitentiary

1875 Mar 3, FF4, Minutes of the Board of Managers, hauling

Cameron, John
1871 Dec, FF4, December Bill for Fees, prisoner
1871 Nov, FF4, November Bill for Fees, prisoner
1871 Oct, FF4, October Bill for Fees, prisoner
1871 Oct 31, FF3, Convicts dismissed from Colorado Penitentiary 13 June 1871 to 1 Dec 1874, prisoner, release no. 15, Crime: larceny, County: Jefferson, Sentence: 1 yr 6 mo, Age: 18, discharged 1873 Feb 16, no remarks
1872 Apr, FF4, April Bill for Fees, prisoner
1872 Dec 31, FF4, Dec Bill for Fees, prisoner
1872 Jan, FF4, January Bill for Fees, prisoner
1872 July, FF4, July Bill for Fees, prisoner
1872, Aug 31, FF4, Aug Bill for Fees, prisoner
1874 Dec 23, FF3, Convicts received at the Colorado State Penitentiary from 13 June 1871 to 1 Dec 1874, Prisoner no. 16, Crime: larceny, County: Jefferson, Sentence: 1 yr 8 mo, Age: 18, Occupation: boot black, 4 11 1/2", Complexion: light, Hair: dk brown, Eyes: blue, Nativity: Canada, Education: reads and writes

Cammeron, Jas
1872 May, FF4, May Bill for Fees, prisoner Canon City Avalanche
1876 Apr 7, FF4, Balance sheet, vendor

Canon City Avalanche
1876 Dec 31, FF4, Report of the Treasurer, vendor
1876 July 10, FF4, Balance sheet, vendor

Canon City Ditch Co
1874 Aug, FF3, Expenditures and Earnings of the Colorado Penitentiary, 2 1/2 days labor
1874 Aug, FF3, Table showing days worked, 2.5
1874 Dec 1, FF4, Balance sheet, vendor
1874 July, FF3, Expenditures and Earnings of the Colorado Penitentiary, 11 1/2 days labor
1874 July, FF3, Table showing days worked, 8.5
1874 June, FF3, Expenditures and Earnings of the Colorado Penitentiary, 28 days labor
1874 May, FF3, Convict Labor Administered by Anson Rudd, 93 1/2 days
1874 May, FF3, Convict Labor Administered by Anson Rudd, 5 7 days
1874 May 29, FF4, Statement of Accounts, water
1875 Dec 6, FF4, Schedule of Open Accounts, vendor

Canon City Times
1876 Apr 7, FF4, Balance sheet, vendor
1876 Dec 31, FF4, Report of the Treasurer, vendor
1876 July 10, FF4, Balance sheet, vendor
1877 Apr 11, FF4, Balance sheet, vendor

Chandler (Cook, Chandler & Barlow)
1874 Dec 1, FF4, Minutes of the Board of Managers, cloth
1874 Dec 1, FF4, Balance sheet, vendor
1874 Nov, FF3, Expenditures and Earnings of the Colorado Penitentiary, cloth
1874 Oct, FF3, Expenditures and Earnings of the Colorado Penitentiary, cloth
1875 Mar 1, FF4, Minutes of the Board of Managers, cloth
1875 Mar 1, FF4, Minutes of the Board of Managers, cloth
1876 Apr 7, FF4, Balance sheet, vendor
1876 Dec 31, FF4, Report of the Treasurer, vendor
1876 Feb 17, FF4, Balance sheet, vendor
1876 Oct 13, FF4, Balance sheet, vendor

Channing, E
1874 Dec 1, FF4, Balance sheet, vendor
1874 Nov, FF3, Expenditures and Earnings of the Colorado Penitentiary, cut stone
1874 Oct, FF3, Expenditures and Earnings of the Colorado Penitentiary, stone

Board of Managers Reports, 1871-1877

1875 Aug 31, FF4, Balance Sheet, vendor
1875 Dec 6, FF4, Schedule of Open Accounts, vendor

Charles, L C
1874 Mar 14, FF4, Letter to the Warden, Clerk
1875 Mar 1, FF4, Minutes of the Board of Managers

Chaves, J G
1872 Dec 31, FF4, Dec Bill for Fees, prisoner

Chaves, Jose Gregorio
1874 Dec 23, FF3, Convicts received at the Colorado State Penitentiary from 13 June 1871 to 1 Dec 1874, Prisoner no. 4, Crime: larceny, County: Las Animas, Sentence: 2 yr, Age: 35, Occupation: farmer, 5 ' 2", Complexion: dark, Hair: black, Eyes: black, Nativity: NM, Education: none

Chavez, I G
1871 Dec, FF4, December Bill for Fees, prisoner
1871 Nov, FF4, November Bill for Fees, prisoner
1871 Oct, FF4, October Bill for Fees, prisoner
1871 Oct 1, FF4, September Bill for Fees, prisoner from Las Animas Cty
1872 Apr, FF4, April Bill for Fees, prisoner
1872 Jan, FF4, January Bill for Fees, prisoner
1872 July, FF4, July Bill for Fees, prisoner
1872 May, FF4, May Bill for Fees, prisoner
1872, Aug 31, FF4, Aug Bill for Fees, prisoner

Chavez, J G
1871 July 8, FF3, Convicts dismissed from Colorado Penitentiary 13 June 1871 to 1 Dec 1874, prisoner, release no. 4, Crime: larceny, County: Las Animas, Sentence: 2 yr, Age: 35, discharged 1873 Mar 6, no remarks

Clark (H C Clark & Co)
1876 Dec 31, FF4, Report of the Treasurer, vendor
1876 Oct 13, FF4, Balance sheet, vendor

Clark, Chas
1874 Dec 1, FF3, Convicts in Colorado Penitentiary on 1 Dec 1874, prisoner, Crime: larceny, County: Arapahoe, Sentence: 1 yr, Age: 16, Occupation: laborer, 5 ' 5 1/2"
1874 Dec 23, FF3, Convicts received at the Colorado State Penitentiary from 13 June 1871 to 1 Dec 1874, Prisoner no. 97, Crime: larceny, County: Arapahoe, Sentence: 1 yr, Age: 16, Occupation: laborer, 5 ' 5 1/2", Complexion: dark, Hair: dark, Eyes: hazel, Nativity: England, Education: reads and writes

Clark, R W
1877 Apr 11, FF4, Balance sheet, vendor

Clellan, James
1874 Aug 31, FF4, Minutes of the Board of Managers, vendor
1874 Dec 1, FF4, Minutes of the Board of Managers, groceries

Clelland, J
1874 Aug, FF3, Expenditures and Earnings of the Colorado Penitentiary, stone
1874 Aug, FF3, Expenditures and Earnings of the Colorado Penitentiary, groceries
1874 July, FF3, Expenditures and Earnings of the Colorado Penitentiary, 32 days labor
1874 May, FF3, Convict Labor Administered by Anson Rudd, 17 days
1874 Oct, FF3, Expenditures and Earnings of the Colorado Penitentiary, groceries
1874 July, FF3, Table showing days worked, 32

Clelland, James
1874 May, FF3, Cash Accounts from the Books of A Rudd
1874 May 29, FF4, Statement of Accounts, shoes
1874 Sept 30, FF3, Cash Accounts of the Colorado Penitentiary
1876 Dec 31, FF4, Report of the Treasurer, vendor
1876 Feb 17, FF4, Balance sheet, vendor

1876 July 10, FF4, Balance sheet, vendor
1876 Oct 13, FF4, Balance sheet, vendor
1877 Apr 11, FF4, Balance sheet, vendor
1877 Jan 1, FF4, Balance sheet, vendor

Clelland, Jas
1874 Dec 1, FF4, Balance sheet, vendor
1874 Nov, FF3, Expenditures and Earnings of the Colorado Penitentiary, groceries
1876 Apr 7, FF4, Balance sheet, vendor

Cole, Jerome
1873 Aug 31, FF4, Aug Bill for Fees, prisoner
1873 July 31, FF4, July Bill for Fees, prisoner
1873 May 3, FF3, Convicts dismissed from Colorado Penitentiary 13 June 1871 to 1 Dec 1874, prisoner, release no. 52, Crime: larceny, County: Jefferson, Sentence: 1 yr 6 mo, Age: 19, discharged 1874 May 19, no remarks
1873 May 31, FF4, May Bill for Fees, prisoner
1874 Dec 23, FF3, Convicts received at the Colorado State Penitentiary from 13 June 1871 to 1 Dec 1874, Prisoner no. 62, Crime: larceny, County: Jefferson, Sentence: 1 yr 6 mo, Age: 19, Occupation: herder, 5 ' 4 1/2", Complexion: light, Hair: sandy, Eyes: brown, Nativity: IA, Education: reads and writes

Collins, J T
1876 Dec 31, FF4, Report of the Treasurer, vendor
1876 Oct 13, FF4, Balance sheet, vendor
1877 Apr 11, FF4, Balance sheet, vendor
1877 Jan 1, FF4, Balance sheet, vendor

Collins, Jno T
1876 Dec 31, FF4, Report of the Treasurer, vendor

Collins, John F
1875 Dec 6, FF4, Schedule of Vouchers Drawn, vendor

Collins, John T
1875 Dec 7, FF4, Minutes of the Board of Managers, vendor
1876 Apr 7, FF4, Balance sheet, vendor

1876 Dec 31, FF4, Report of the Treasurer, vendor
1876 Feb 17, FF4, Balance sheet, vendor
1876 July 10, FF4, Balance sheet, vendor

Considine, P W
1874 Dec 1, FF4, Minutes of the Board of Managers, hauling sand

Constantine, P W
1874 Oct, FF3, Expenditures and Earnings of the Colorado Penitentiary, hauling

Cook & Co
1874 July, FF3, Expenditures and Earnings of the Colorado Penitentiary, painting sign

Cook, Chandler & Barlow
1874 Dec 1, FF4, Minutes of the Board of Managers, cloth
1874 Dec 1, FF4, Balance sheet, vendor
1874 Nov, FF3, Expenditures and Earnings of the Colorado Penitentiary, cloth
1874 Oct, FF3, Expenditures and Earnings of the Colorado Penitentiary, cloth
1875 June 4, FF4, Minutes of the Board of Managers, vendor
1875 Mar 1, FF4, Minutes of the Board of Managers, cloth
1875 Mar 1, FF4, Minutes of the Board of Managers, cloth
1876 Apr 7, FF4, Balance sheet, vendor
1876 Dec 31, FF4, Report of the Treasurer, vendor
1876 Feb 17, FF4, Balance sheet, vendor
1876 Oct 13, FF4, Balance sheet, vendor

Cook, G W
1874 Sept 19, FF3, Cash Accounts of the Colorado Penitentiary

Cook, Geo
1871 Aug 5, FF3, Convicts dismissed from Colorado Penitentiary 13 June 1871 to 1 Dec 1874, prisoner, release no. 13, Crime: larceny, County: Arapahoe, Sentence: 2 yr, Age: 24, discharged 1873 Apr 29, no remarks

Cook, Geo W
1874 Aug, FF3, Expenditures and Earnings of the Colorado Penitentiary, meat

1874 Aug 31, FF4, Minutes of the Board of Managers, vendor

Cook, George
1871 Dec, FF4, December Bill for Fees, prisoner
1871 Nov, FF4, November Bill for Fees, prisoner
1872 Apr, FF4, April Bill for Fees, prisoner
1872 Dec 31, FF4, Dec Bill for Fees, prisoner
1872 Jan, FF4, January Bill for Fees, prisoner
1872 July, FF4, July Bill for Fees, prisoner
1872 May, FF4, May Bill for Fees, prisoner
1872, Aug 31, FF4, Aug Bill for Fees, prisoner
1873 Apr 30, FF4, April Bill for Fees, prisoner
1874 Dec 23, FF3, Convicts received at the Colorado State Penitentiary from 13 June 1871 to 1 Dec 1874, Prisoner no. 14, Crime: larceny, County: Arapahoe, Sentence: 2 yr, Age: 24, Occupation: clerk, 5 ' 9", Complexion: light, Hair: dk brown, Eyes: brown, Nativity: NJ, Education: reads and writes

Cott, George
1873 Aug 31, FF4, Aug Bill for Fees, prisoner
1874 Dec 1, FF3, Convicts in Colorado Penitentiary on 1 Dec 1874, prisoner, Crime: larceny, County: Weld, Sentence: 2 yr, Age: 23, Occupation: farmer, 5 ' 7 1/2"
1874 Dec 23, FF3, Convicts received at the Colorado State Penitentiary from 13 June 1871 to 1 Dec 1874, Prisoner no. 71, Crime: larceny, County: Weld, Sentence: 2 yr, Age: 23, Occupation: farmer, 5 ' 7 1/2", Complexion: light, Hair: light, Eyes: grey, Nativity: IN, Education: reads and writes

County Road
1874 Aug, FF3, Table showing days worked, 142.5
1874 Aug, FF3, Expenditures and Earnings of the Colorado Penitentiary, 142 1/2 days labor

1874 July, FF3, Table showing days worked, 98
1874 July, FF3, Expenditures and Earnings of the Colorado Penitentiary, 98 days labor
1874 Nov, FF3, Table showing days worked, 36
1874 Nov, FF3, Expenditures and Earnings of the Colorado Penitentiary, 36 days labor
1874 Oct, FF3, Table showing days worked, 267
1874 Oct, FF3, Expenditures and Earnings of the Colorado Penitentiary, 259 days labor
1874 Sept, FF3, Table showing days worked, 86
1874 Sept, FF3, Expenditures and Earnings of the Colorado Penitentiary, 86 days labor

Crampton, W H
1875 Dec 6, FF4, Schedule of Open Accounts, vendor

Craven, T H
1874 Aug 3, FF3, Cash Accounts of the Colorado Penitentiary
1876 Dec 31, FF4, Report of the Treasurer, vendor
1876 Oct 13, FF4, Balance sheet, vendor

Craven, Th H
1874 July, FF3, Expenditures and Earnings of the Colorado Penitentiary, stone

Culver, Page & Hoyne
1876 Dec 31, FF4, Report of the Treasurer, vendor
1877 Jan 1, FF4, Balance sheet, vendor

Currier, Geo W
1877 Apr 11, FF4, Balance sheet, vendor

Curtice (Alling, Curtice & Co)
1876 Dec 31, FF4, Report of the Treasurer, vendor

Curtis (Alling Curtis & Co)
1876 Feb 17, FF4, Balance sheet, vendor

Colorado Territorial Penitentiary

D

Dailey, William
1873 July 31, FF4, July Bill for Fees, prisoner

Dailey, Wm
1874 Dec 1, FF3, Convicts in Colorado Penitentiary on 1 Dec 1874, prisoner, Crime: robbery, County: Arapahoe, Sentence: 3 yr, Age: 25, Occupation: laborer, 5 ' 10"

Daily, Dennis
1872 Apr, FF4, April Bill for Fees, prisoner
1872 Jan 3, FF3, Convicts dismissed from Colorado Penitentiary 13 June 1871 to 1 Dec 1874, prisoner, release no. 23, Crime: larceny, County: Weld, Sentence: 1 yr, Age: 22, discharged 1872 Nov 20, no remarks
1872 July, FF4, July Bill for Fees, prisoner
1872 May, FF4, May Bill for Fees, prisoner
1872, Aug 31, FF4, Aug Bill for Fees, prisoner
1874 Dec 23, FF3, Convicts received at the Colorado State Penitentiary from 13 June 1871 to 1 Dec 1874, Prisoner no. 28, Crime: larceny, County: Weld, Sentence: 1 yr, Age: 22, Occupation: machinist, 5 ' 7", Complexion: dark, Hair: black, Eyes: grey, Nativity: NY, Education: reads and writes

Daily, William
1873 Aug 31, FF4, Aug Bill for Fees, prisoner
1873 June 30, FF4, June Bill for Fees, prisoner

Daily, Wm
1874 Dec 1, FF3, Convicts Escaped since Organization of the Prison, escapee no. 12, Crime: robbery, County: Arapahoe, Sentence: 3 yr, Age: 25, received 1873 June 25, escaped 1874 Sept 30, recaptured same day
1874 Dec 23, FF3, Convicts received at the Colorado State Penitentiary from 13 June 1871 to 1 Dec 1874, Prisoner no. 67, Crime: robbery, County: Arapahoe, Sentence: 3 yr, Age: 25, Occupation: laborer, 5 ' 10", Complexion: dark, Hair: dark, Eyes: blue, Nativity: NY, Education: reads and writes

Daley, Dennis
1872 Jan, FF4, January Bill for Fees, prisoner

Daniels Fisher & Co
1876 Dec 31, FF4, Report of the Treasurer, vendor
1877 Jan 1, FF4, Balance sheet, vendor

Daugherty, Dan'l
1874 Dec 23, FF3, Convicts received at the Colorado State Penitentiary from 13 June 1871 to 1 Dec 1874, Prisoner no. 23, Crime: abortion, County: Gilpin, Sentence: 1 yr, Age: 22, Occupation: lawyer, 5 ' 5", Complexion: florid, Hair: dk brown, Eyes: blue, Nativity: ME, Education: reads and writes

Davids, C N
1876 Dec 31, FF4, Report of the Treasurer, vendor
1876 Oct 13, FF4, Balance sheet, vendor
1877 Apr 11, FF4, Balance sheet, vendor
1877 Jan 1, FF4, Balance sheet, vendor

Davids, Chauncey N
1876 Dec 31, FF4, Report of the Treasurer, vendor
1876 July 10, FF4, Balance sheet, vendor

Davis, C M
1876 Dec 31, FF4, Report of the Treasurer, vendor

Davis, Chas
1875 Mar 1, FF4, Minutes of the Board of Managers, Guard

D

Dawson, J W
1876 Apr 7, FF4, Balance sheet, vendor
1876 Dec 31, FF4, Report of the Treasurer, vendor

Dean, Charles
1872 Dec 31, FF4, Dec Bill for Fees, prisoner

Board of Managers Reports, 1871-1877

1872 July, FF4, July Bill for Fees, prisoner
1872 May, FF4, May Bill for Fees, prisoner
1872, Aug 31, FF4, Aug Bill for Fees, prisoner
1873 Apr 30, FF4, April Bill for Fees, prisoner
1873 Aug 31, FF4, Aug Bill for Fees, prisoner
1873 July 31, FF4, July Bill for Fees, prisoner
1873 June 30, FF4, June Bill for Fees, prisoner
1873 May 31, FF4, May Bill for Fees, prisoner

Dean, Chas
1872 May 21, FF3, Convicts dismissed from Colorado Penitentiary 13 June 1871 to 1 Dec 1874, prisoner, release no. 30, Crime: larceny, County: Arapahoe, Sentence: 1 yr 6 mo, Age: 20, discharged 1872 Aug 5, no remarks
1874 Dec 23, FF3, Convicts received at the Colorado State Penitentiary from 13 June 1871 to 1 Dec 1874, Prisoner no. 37, Crime: larceny, County: Arapahoe, Sentence: 1 yr 8 mo, Age: 20, Occupation: laborer, 5 ' 5 1/2", Complexion: colored, Hair: black, Eyes: black, Nativity: MD, Education: reads and writes

Deanson, Dan
1872 May, FF4, May Bill for Fees, prisoner

Decker (Symes & Decker)
1876 Dec 31, FF4, Report of the Treasurer, vendor

Denver & Rio Grande Railway Co
1874 Aug 31, FF4, Minutes of the Board of Managers, vendor
1874 Dec 1, FF4, Minutes of the Board of Managers, freight
1874 Dec 1, FF4, Balance sheet, vendor
1875 Aug 31, FF4, Balance Sheet, vendor
1875 Dec 6, FF4, Schedule of Vouchers Drawn, vendor
1875 Dec 7, FF4, Minutes of the Board of Managers, vendor

1875 June 4, FF4, Minutes of the Board of Managers, vendor
1875 Mar 3, FF4, Minutes of the Board of Managers, coal
1876 Apr 7, FF4, Balance sheet, vendor
1876 Dec 31, FF4, Report of the Treasurer, vendor
1876 July 10, FF4, Balance sheet, vendor
1876 Oct 13, FF4, Balance sheet, vendor
1877 Apr 11, FF4, Balance sheet, vendor
1877 Jan 1, FF4, Balance sheet, vendor

Denver and Rio Grande Railroad Company
1874 Nov, FF3, Expenditures and Earnings of the Colorado Penitentiary, freight
1874 Nov 16, FF3, Cash accounts
1874 Oct, FF3, Expenditures and Earnings of the Colorado Penitentiary, coal
1874 Oct, FF3, Expenditures and Earnings of the Colorado Penitentiary, freight
1874 Sept, FF3, Expenditures and Earnings of the Colorado Penitentiary, freight
1874 Sept 30, FF3, Cash Accounts of the Colorado Penitentiary

Denver Brewing Co
1876 Dec 31, FF4, Report of the Treasurer, vendor
1877 Jan 1, FF4, Balance sheet, vendor

Denver Tribune
1874 Aug 31, FF4, Minutes of the Board of Managers, vendor
1874 July, FF3, Expenditures and Earnings of the Colorado Penitentiary, printing
1874 June, FF3, Expenditures and Earnings of the Colorado Penitentiary, printing
1874 Sept 10, FF3, Cash Accounts of the Colorado Penitentiary
1875 Mar 1, FF4, Minutes of the Board of Managers, printing
1876 Apr 7, FF4, Balance sheet, vendor
1876 Dec 31, FF4, Report of the Treasurer, vendor
1876 July 10, FF4, Balance sheet, vendor
1876 Oct 13, FF4, Balance sheet, vendor
1877 Apr 11, FF4, Balance sheet, vendor

Colorado Territorial Penitentiary

Diamond, Dan'l
 1872 Dec 31, FF4, Dec Bill for Fees, prisoner
 1872 July, FF4, July Bill for Fees, prisoner
 1872, Aug 31, FF4, Aug Bill for Fees, prisoner

Dimming, James
 1876 Oct 13, FF4, Balance sheet, vendor

Dimon, Dan
 1872 May 21, FF3, Convicts dismissed from Colorado Penitentiary 13 June 1871 to 1 Dec 1874, prisoner, release no. 31, Crime: larceny, County: Arapahoe, Sentence: 1 yr, Age: 26, discharged 1873 Mar 17, no remarks
 1874 Dec 23, FF3, Convicts received at the Colorado State Penitentiary from 13 June 1871 to 1 Dec 1874, Prisoner no. 38, Crime: larceny, County: Arapahoe, Sentence: 1 yr, Age: 25, Occupation: laborer, 5 3/4", Complexion: colored, Hair: black, Eyes: dk brown, Nativity: OH, Education: none

Dodge, F
 1872 Jan, FF4, January Bill for Fees, prisoner

Dodge, F
 1872 May, FF4, May Bill for Fees, prisoner

Dodge, Frank
 1871 Dec, FF4, December Bill for Fees, prisoner
 1871 July 9, FF3, Convicts dismissed from Colorado Penitentiary 13 June 1871 to 1 Dec 1874, prisoner, release no. 12, Crime: larceny, County: Arapahoe, Sentence: 2 yr, Age: 30, discharged 1873 Feb 19, no remarks
 1871 Nov, FF4, November Bill for Fees, prisoner
 1871 Oct, FF4, October Bill for Fees, prisoner
 1871 Oct 1, FF4, September Bill for Fees, prisoner
 1872 Apr, FF4, April Bill for Fees, prisoner
 1872 Dec 31, FF4, Dec Bill for Fees, prisoner
 1872 July, FF4, July Bill for Fees, prisoner
 1872, Aug 31, FF4, Aug Bill for Fees, prisoner
 1874 Dec 23, FF3, Convicts received at the Colorado State Penitentiary from 13 June 1871 to 1 Dec 1874, Prisoner no. 13, Crime: forgery & larceny, County: Arapahoe, Sentence: 2 yr, Age: 30, Occupation: clerk, 5 ' 7 1/2", Complexion: dark, Hair: brown, Eyes: blue, Nativity: NY, Education: reads and writes

Doherty, Daniel
 1871 Dec, FF4, December Bill for Fees, prisoner
 1871 Nov, FF4, November Bill for Fees, prisoner
 1872 Apr, FF4, April Bill for Fees, prisoner
 1872 Jan, FF4, January Bill for Fees, prisoner
 1872 July 1, FF4, July Bill for Fees, pardoned
 1872 May, FF4, May Bill for Fees, prisoner

Doolittle, J K
 1876 Dec 31, FF4, Report of the Treasurer, vendor

Doughterty, Danl
 1871 Nov 4, FF3, Convicts dismissed from Colorado Penitentiary 13 June 1871 to 1 Dec 1874, prisoner, release no. 19, Crime: abortionist, County: Gilpin, Sentence: 1 yr, Age: 22, discharged 1872 July 13, pardoned by ____

Douglas & Co
 1877 Jan 1, FF4, Balance sheet, vendor

Douglass & Co
 1876 Dec 31, FF4, Report of the Treasurer, vendor

Dowling, Fred
 1874 Dec 1, FF3, Convicts Escaped since Organization of the Prison, escapee no. 10, Crime: robbery, County: Jefferson, Sentence: 10 yr, Age: 25, received 1873 June 20, escaped 1874 May 26, recaptured 11 June 1874
 1874 Dec 1, FF3, Convicts in Colorado Penitentiary on 1 Dec 1874, prisoner,

Crime: robbery, County: Jefferson, Sentence: 10 yr, Age: 25, Occupation: laborer, 5 ' 8"

1874 Dec 23, FF3, Convicts received at the Colorado State Penitentiary from 13 June 1871 to 1 Dec 1874, Prisoner no. 64, Crime: robbery, County: Jefferson, Sentence: 10 yr, Age: 25, Occupation: laborer, 5 ' 8", Complexion: light, Hair: sandy, Eyes: blue, Nativity: VA, Education: reads and writes

Dowling, Frederick

1873 Aug 31, FF4, Aug Bill for Fees, prisoner

1873 July 31, FF4, July Bill for Fees, prisoner

1873 June 30, FF4, June Bill for Fees, prisoner

E

Eaton, B F

1874 Aug 31, FF4, Minutes of the Board of Managers, Board Member

1874 Dec 1, FF4, Minutes of the Board of Managers, Board Member

1875 Mar 1, FF4, Minutes of the Board of Managers, Board Member

1875 Mar 3, FF4, Minutes of the Board of Managers, Board Member

Eaton, B H

1875 Sept 2, FF4, Minutes of the Board of Managers, Board Member

1876 Dec 31, FF4, Report of the Treasurer, Treasurer of the Board of Managers

Eaton, B N

1876 Dec 31, FF4, Report of the Treasurer, Board Mgr

Eaton, Mr

1875 Dec 7, FF4, Minutes of the Board of Managers, Board Member

1875 June 1, FF4, Minutes of the Board of Managers, Board Member

1875 June 4, FF4, Minutes of the Board of Managers, Board Member

Engleman & Co

1874 Aug, FF3, Expenditures and Earnings of the Colorado Penitentiary, stone

1874 Dec 1, FF4, Balance sheet, vendor

1874 June, FF3, Cash Accounts from the Books of A Rudd

1874 June, FF3, Expenditures and Earnings of the Colorado Penitentiary, clothing

1874 May, FF3, Cash Accounts from the Books of A Rudd

1874 May 29, FF4, Statement of Accounts, shoes, clothing

1874 May 29, FF4, Statement of Accounts, dry goods and shoes

1874 Sept 15, FF3, Cash Accounts of the Colorado Penitentiary

1875 Dec 6, FF4, Schedule of Vouchers Drawn, vendor

1875 Dec 7, FF4, Minutes of the Board of Managers, vendor

1875 Mar 3, FF4, Minutes of the Board of Managers, clothing

1876 Apr 7, FF4, Balance sheet, vendor

1876 Dec 31, FF4, Report of the Treasurer, vendor

1876 Feb 17, FF4, Balance sheet, vendor

1876 July 10, FF4, Balance sheet, vendor

1876 Oct 13, FF4, Balance sheet, vendor

1877 Apr 11, FF4, Balance sheet, vendor

1877 Jan 1, FF4, Balance sheet, vendor

Engleman (M M Engleman & Co)

1876 Dec 31, FF4, Report of the Treasurer, vendor

F

Fairfield Woolen Mills

1876 Dec 31, FF4, Report of the Treasurer, vendor

1877 Jan 1, FF4, Balance sheet, vendor

Ferrler, W R

1874 May 29, FF4, Statement of Accounts, straw

Fink, J W

1876 Dec 31, FF4, Report of the Treasurer, vendor

Colorado Territorial Penitentiary

Fisher (Daniels Fisher & Co)
1876 Dec 31, FF4, Report of the Treasurer, vendor
1877 Jan 1, FF4, Balance sheet, vendor

Fitch, James H
1874 Dec 23, FF3, Convicts received at the Colorado State Penitentiary from 13 June 1871 to 1 Dec 1874, Prisoner no. 91, Crime: murder, County: Bent, Sentence: life, Age: 34, Occupation: saloon keeper, 5 ' 5 1/2", Complexion: ight, Hair: brown, Eyes: blue, Nativity: IL, Education: reads and writes

Fitch, Jas H
1874 Dec 1, FF3, Convicts in Colorado Penitentiary on 1 Dec 1874, prisoner, Crime: murder, County: Bent, Sentence: life, Age: 34, Occupation: saloon keeper, 5 ' 5 1/2"

Force, R Y
1876 Apr 7, FF4, Balance sheet, vendor
1876 Dec 31, FF4, Report of the Treasurer, vendor

Ford, J B
1872 Apr, FF4, April Bill for Fees, prisoner

Ford, John B
1872 Dec 31, FF4, Dec Bill for Fees, prisoner
1872 Jan, FF4, January Bill for Fees, prisoner
1872 Jan 10, FF3, Convicts dismissed from Colorado Penitentiary 13 June 1871 to 1 Dec 1874, prisoner, release no. 25, Crime: attempt to murder, County: Boulder, Sentence: 1 yr 6 mo, Age: 28, discharged 1873 June 24, no remarks
1872 July, FF4, July Bill for Fees, prisoner
1872 May, FF4, May Bill for Fees, prisoner
1872, Aug 31, FF4, Aug Bill for Fees, prisoner
1873 Apr 30, FF4, April Bill for Fees, prisoner
1874 Dec 1, FF3, Convicts Escaped since Organization of the Prison, escapee no. 6, Crime: assault to kill, County: Boulder, Sentence: 1 yr 6 mo, Age: 28, received 1872 Jan 10, escaped 1872 Nov 12, recaptured same day
1874 Dec 23, FF3, Convicts received at the Colorado State Penitentiary from 13 June 1871 to 1 Dec 1874, Prisoner no. 31, Crime: assault with intent to commit murder, County: Boulder, Sentence: 1 yr 8 mo, Age: 28, Occupation: stone mason, 6 ' 1/2", Complexion: light, Hair: dk brown, Eyes: blue, Nativity: NY, Education: reads and writes

Fowler, W R
1874 Sept, FF3, Expenditures and Earnings of the Colorado Penitentiary, hay
1874 Sept 28, FF3, Cash Accounts of the Colorado Penitentiary
1875 Mar 1, FF4, Minutes of the Board of Managers, straw
1876 Dec 31, FF4, Report of the Treasurer, vendor
1876 Feb 17, FF4, Balance sheet, vendor
1877 Jan 1, FF4, Balance sheet, vendor

Fox, Moses
1873 Apr 30, FF4, April Bill for Fees, prisoner
1873 Aug 31, FF4, Aug Bill for Fees, prisoner
1873 Jan 25, FF3, Convicts dismissed from Colorado Penitentiary 13 June 1871 to 1 Dec 1874, prisoner, release no. 46, Crime: murder, County: El Paso, Sentence: 2 yr, Age: 26, discharged 1874 Sept 29, pardoned by Act Gov Jenkins
1873 July 31, FF4, July Bill for Fees, prisoner
1873 June 30, FF4, June Bill for Fees, prisoner
1873 May 31, FF4, May Bill for Fees, prisoner
1874 Dec 23, FF3, Convicts received at the Colorado State Penitentiary from 13 June 1871 to 1 Dec 1874, Prisoner no. 55, Crime: murder, County: El Paso, Sentence: 2 yr, Age: 26, Occupation: farmer, 5 ' 11", Complexion: dark,

Hair: auburn, Eyes: grey, Nativity: PA, Education: reads and writes

Frank, J W
1876 Feb 17, FF4, Balance sheet, vendor

Frazier, J F
1874 July 24, FF3, Cash Accounts of the Colorado Penitentiary

Frazier, R J
1877 Apr 11, FF4, Balance sheet, vendor

Frazier, T J
1874 Dec 31, FF4, Expenses paid for G W Graham & Switterline, US Prisoners, nurse at Rosita

Frost, Frank
1874 Dec 1, FF3, Convicts Escaped since Organization of the Prison, escapee no. 18, Crime: larceny, County: Arapahoe, Sentence: 3 yr, Age: 27, received 1874 June 9, escaped 1874 Nov 4
1874 Dec 23, FF3, Convicts received at the Colorado State Penitentiary from 13 June 1871 to 1 Dec 1874, Prisoner no. 88, Crime: larceny, County: Arapahoe, Sentence: 3 yr, Age: 27, Occupation: arness maker, 5 ' 7 1/2", Complexion: light, Hair: lt brown, Eyes: blue, Nativity: NY, Education: reads and writes

Fry, J S
1874 Dec 31, FF4, Expenses paid for G W Graham & Switterline, US Prisoners, boarding prisoner at Rosita
1874 July 24, FF3, Cash Accounts of the Colorado Penitentiary

G

Gano & Thomas
1876 Dec 31, FF4, Report of the Treasurer, vendor
1877 Jan 1, FF4, Balance sheet, vendor

Garcia, Jesus M
1874 Dec 1, FF3, Convicts in Colorado Penitentiary on 1 Dec 1874, prisoner, Crime: larceny, County: Fremont, Sentence: 2 yr, Age: 18, Occupation: laborer, 5 ' 8"
1874 Dec 23, FF3, Convicts received at the Colorado State Penitentiary from 13 June 1871 to 1 Dec 1874, Prisoner no. 86, Crime: larceny, County: Fremont, Sentence: 2 yr, Age: 18, Occupation: laborer, 5 ' 8", Complexion: light, Hair: black, Eyes: brown, Nativity: NM, Education: none

Gill, N
1877 Apr 11, FF4, Balance sheet, vendor

Gill, Rev
1876 Dec 31, FF4, Report of the Treasurer, vendor

Gill, Rev W
1876 Dec 31, FF4, Report of the Treasurer, vendor

Gill, Rev Wm
1876 Oct 13, FF4, Balance sheet, vendor

Gill, Wm
1877 Jan 1, FF4, Balance sheet, vendor

Gilland, A
1874 May, FF3, Cash Accounts from the Books of A Rudd

Gilliland, A J
1874 May 29, FF4, Statement of Accounts, wood, hauling services
1874 May 29, FF4, Statement of Accounts, plowing garden

Gore, C & Co
1874 May, FF3, Cash Accounts from the Books of A Rudd

Gove, C & Co
1874 May 29, FF4, Statement of Accounts, pistols, ammunition

Grading
1874 Nov, FF3, Table showing days worked, 109

Graham, G W
1875 Jan 1, FF4, Bill for G W Graham, escaped prisoner

Graham, Geo W
1874 Dec 1, FF3, Convicts in Colorado Penitentiary on 1 Dec 1874, prisoner,

Crime: conspiracy, County: Arapahoe, Sentence: 2 yr, Age: 33, Occupation: soldier, 6 ' 1"
1874 Dec 1, FF3, Convicts Escaped since Organization of the Prison, escapee no. 15, Crime: conspiracy, County: Arapahoe, Sentence: 2 yr, Age: 33, received
1873 Dec 3, escaped 1874 May 26, recaptured 10 June 1874
1874 Dec 23, FF3, Convicts received at the Colorado State Penitentiary from 13 June 1871 to 1 Dec 1874, Prisoner no. 75, Crime: conspiracy, County: Arapahoe, Sentence: 2 yr, Age: 33, Occupation: soldier, 6 ' 1", Complexion: florid, Hair: dk brown, Eyes: grey, Nativity: NC, Education: reads and writes

Graham, Joseph
1875 Mar 1, FF4, Minutes of the Board of Managers, Guard

Grazier, T J
1875 Jan 1, FF4, Bill for G W Graham, nurse at Rosita

Green, H H R
1875 June 4, FF4, Minutes of the Board of Managers, vendor

Green, Marmaduke
1871 Dec 2, FF4, Auditor's Letter, Commissioner
1871 Dec 31, FF4, Auditor's Letter, Commissioner
1871 Nov 7, FF4, Auditor's Letter, Commissioner
1871 Oct 5, FF4, Auditor's Letter, Commissioner

Greenwood, W H
1874 Aug, FF3, Expenditures and Earnings of the Colorado Penitentiary, stone
1874 Nov 2, FF3, Cash Accounts of the Colorado Penitentiary
1874 Sept, FF3, Expenditures and Earnings of the Colorado Penitentiary, stone

Grey, Herbert
1875 Sept 1, FF4, Schedule of Vouchers Drawn, Guard
1876 Dec 31, FF4, Report of the Treasurer, vendor

Griffin Ditch
1874 May, FF3, Convict Labor Administered by Anson Rudd, 8 days

Griffin, Benj
1874 Dec 1, FF4, Balance sheet, vendor
1875 Aug 31, FF4, Balance Sheet, vendor
1875 Dec 6, FF4, Schedule of Open Accounts, vendor

Gry, J S
1875 Jan 1, FF4, Bill for G W Graham, Board at Rosita

H

Haftaben, Charles
1871 Oct 1, FF4, September Bill for Fees, prisoner from Pueblo Cty
1872 Apr, FF4, April Bill for Fees, prisoner
1872 Jan, FF4, January Bill for Fees, prisoner
1872 May, FF4, May Bill for Fees, prisoner

Hagar & Co
1874 Aug, FF3, Expenditures and Earnings of the Colorado Penitentiary, 130 1/2 days labor
1874 Aug, FF3, Expenditures and Earnings of the Colorado Penitentiary, merchandise
1874 Sept 14, FF3, Cash Accounts of the Colorado Penitentiary

Hagar (A J Hagar & Co)
1874 Sept, FF3, Expenditures and Earnings of the Colorado Penitentiary, 286 1/2 days labor

Hager & Co
1874 Dec 1, FF4, Balance sheet, vendor
1875 Aug 31, FF4, Balance Sheet, vendor
1875 Dec 6, FF4, Schedule of Open Accounts, vendor

Hager & Co Mill Ditch
  1874 Aug, FF3, Table showing days worked, 130.5
  1874 Sept, FF3, Table showing days worked, 286.5

Hager (A J Hager & Co)
  1874 Oct, FF3, Expenditures and Earnings of the Colorado Penitentiary, flour

Hailey, Levi
  1874 June, FF3, Cash Accounts from the Books of A Rudd, wood
  1874 May 29, FF4, Statement of Accounts, wood

Hall, Charles J
  1875 Dec 7, FF4, Minutes of the Board of Managers, vendor

Hall, Harry I
  1872 July, FF4, July Bill for Fees, prisoner
  1872, Aug 31, FF4, Aug Bill for Fees, prisoner

Hall, Harry J
  1872 Feb 7, FF3, Convicts dismissed from Colorado Penitentiary 13 June 1871 to 1 Dec 1874, prisoner, release no. 29, Crime: robbing the US Mail, County: Arapahoe, Sentence: 2 yr, Age: 26, discharged 1873 Jan 20, no remarks
  1874 Dec 23, FF3, Convicts received at the Colorado State Penitentiary from 13 June 1871 to 1 Dec 1874, Prisoner no. 35, Crime: embezzling from the US Mail, County: Arapahoe, Sentence: 2 yr, Age: 26, Occupation: machinist, 5' 7", Complexion: light, Hair: dk brown, Eyes: blue, Nativity: IA, Education: reads and writes

Hall, W H
  1876 Dec 31, FF4, Report of the Treasurer, vendor
  1877 Apr 11, FF4, Balance sheet, vendor

Harlupe, W N
  1877 Apr 11, FF4, Balance sheet, vendor

Harper & Weston
  1874 Nov 12, FF3, Cash Accounts of the Colorado Penitentiary

  1874 Sept, FF3, Expenditures and Earnings of the Colorado Penitentiary, stone

Harris, Nathan
  1871 Dec, FF4, December Bill for Fees, prisoner
  1871 Nov, FF4, November Bill for Fees, prisoner
  1871 Oct, FF4, October Bill for Fees, prisoner
  1871 Oct 31, FF3, Convicts dismissed from Colorado Penitentiary 13 June 1871 to 1 Dec 1874, prisoner, release no. 14, Crime: larceny, County: Jefferson, Sentence: 3 yr, Age: 24, discharged 1873 Nov 23, pardoned by ____
  1872 Apr, FF4, April Bill for Fees, prisoner
  1872 Dec 31, FF4, Dec Bill for Fees, prisoner
  1872 Jan, FF4, January Bill for Fees, prisoner
  1872 July, FF4, July Bill for Fees, prisoner
  1872 May, FF4, May Bill for Fees, prisoner
  1872, Aug 31, FF4, Aug Bill for Fees, prisoner
  1873 Apr 30, FF4, April Bill for Fees, prisoner
  1873 Aug 31, FF4, Aug Bill for Fees, prisoner
  1873 July 31, FF4, July Bill for Fees, prisoner
  1873 June 30, FF4, June Bill for Fees, prisoner
  1873 May 31, FF4, May Bill for Fees, prisoner
  1874 Dec 23, FF3, Convicts received at the Colorado State Penitentiary from 13 June 1871 to 1 Dec 1874, Prisoner no. 15, Crime: larceny, County: Jefferson, Sentence: 3 yr, Age: 24, Occupation: clerk, 5' 8 1/2", Complexion: light, Hair: lt brown, Eyes: blue, Nativity: Asia, Education: reads and writes

Harris, William
  1872 July, FF4, July Bill for Fees, prisoner
  1872 May, FF4, May Bill for Fees, prisoner
  1872, Aug 31, FF4, Aug Bill for Fees, prisoner

Colorado Territorial Penitentiary

Harris, Wm
1871 Nov 4, FF3, Convicts dismissed from Colorado Penitentiary 13 June 1871 to 1 Dec 1874, prisoner, release no. 16, Crime: larceny, County: Arapahoe, Sentence: 1 yr, Age: 28, discharged 1872 Sept 18, one month good time
1871 Dec, FF4, December Bill for Fees, prisoner
1871 Nov, FF4, November Bill for Fees, prisoner
1872 Apr, FF4, April Bill for Fees, prisoner
1872 Jan, FF4, January Bill for Fees, prisoner
1874 Dec 23, FF3, Convicts received at the Colorado State Penitentiary from 13 June 1871 to 1 Dec 1874, Prisoner no. 18, Crime: larceny, County: Arapahoe, Sentence: 5 yr, Age: 28, Occupation: cook, 5 ' 10 1/2", Complexion: dark, Hair: black, Eyes: black, Nativity: NJ, Education: reads and writes

Harrison (Prentiss & Harrison)
1874 Dec 1, FF4, Balance sheet, vendor
1875 Aug 31, FF4, Balance Sheet, vendor
1875 Dec 6, FF4, Schedule of Open Accounts, vendor

Harrison, I H
1876 Oct 13, FF4, Balance sheet, vendor
1876 Apr 7, FF4, Balance sheet, vendor
1876 Dec 31, FF4, Report of the Treasurer, vendor
1876 Feb 17, FF4, Balance sheet, vendor
1876 July 10, FF4, Balance sheet, vendor

Harrupe, W N
1876 Oct 13, FF4, Balance sheet, vendor

Harterfeel, WM
1876 July 10, FF4, Balance sheet, vendor

Hartessee, W M
1876 Dec 31, FF4, Report of the Treasurer, vendor

Hartessee, Wm H
1876 Dec 31, FF4, Report of the Treasurer, vendor

Hartissee, Wm
1876 Dec 31, FF4, Report of the Treasurer, vendor

Hartupe, Wm
1877 Jan 1, FF4, Balance sheet, vendor

Hartusse, W
1875 Dec 6, FF4, Schedule of Vouchers Drawn, vendor

Hartussee, William
1875 Dec 7, FF4, Minutes of the Board of Managers, vendor

Hartwell, F
1874 Oct, FF3, Expenditures and Earnings of the Colorado Penitentiary, sharpening tools
1874 Sept, FF3, Expenditures and Earnings of the Colorado Penitentiary, stone

Hayes, Phillip
1876 Dec 31, FF4, Report of the Treasurer, vendor
1876 July 10, FF4, Balance sheet, vendor

Hays, James
1874 Dec 1, FF3, Convicts in Colorado Penitentiary on 1 Dec 1874, prisoner, Crime: larceny, County: Arapahoe, Sentence: 1 yr 6 mo, Age: 36, Occupation: laborer, 5 ' 7"
1874 Dec 23, FF3, Convicts received at the Colorado State Penitentiary from 13 June 1871 to 1 Dec 1874, Prisoner no. 82, Crime: larceny, County: Arapahoe, Sentence: 1 yr 6 mo, Age: 36, Occupation: laborer, 5 ' 7", Complexion: dark, Hair: dark, Eyes: blue, Nativity: Ireland, Education: reads only

Hays, Phillip
1876 Apr 7, FF4, Balance sheet, vendor
1876 Feb 17, FF4, Balance sheet, vendor

Heller, Charles
1872 Apr, FF4, April Bill for Fees, prisoner
1872 July, FF4, July Bill for Fees, prisoner

Heller, George
1872 May, FF4, May Bill for Fees, prisoner

Board of Managers Reports, 1871-1877

Helm, W A
   1874 May, FF3, Convict Labor Administered by Anson Rudd, 3 days
   1874 Oct 24, FF3, Cash accounts

Hemerle, Paul
   1875 Dec 6, FF4, Schedule of Open Accounts, vendor

Henderson, W H
   1871 Dec, FF4, December Bill for Fees, prisoner

Henderson, William H
   1872 Dec 31, FF4, Dec Bill for Fees, prisoner
   1872 July, FF4, July Bill for Fees, prisoner
   1873 Apr 30, FF4, April Bill for Fees, prisoner
   1873 May 31, FF4, May Bill for Fees, prisoner

Henderson, Wm
   1872 Apr, FF4, April Bill for Fees, prisoner

Henderson, Wm H
   1871 June 13, FF3, Convicts dismissed from Colorado Penitentiary 13 June 1871 to 1 Dec 1874, prisoner, release no. 2, Crime: manslaughter, County: Clear Creek, Sentence: 5 yr, Age: 35, discharged 1874 Sept 9, pardoned by Gov McCook
   1871 Nov, FF4, November Bill for Fees, prisoner
   1871 Oct, FF4, October Bill for Fees, prisoner
   1871 Oct 1, FF4, September Bill for Fees, prisoner from Clear Creek Cty
   1872 Jan, FF4, January Bill for Fees, prisoner
   1872 May, FF4, May Bill for Fees, prisoner
   1872, Aug 31, FF4, Aug Bill for Fees, prisoner
   1872 Jan, FF4, January Bill for Fees, prisoner
   1872 May, FF4, May Bill for Fees, prisoner
   1873 Aug 31, FF4, Aug Bill for Fees, prisoner
   1873 July 31, FF4, July Bill for Fees, prisoner
   1873 June 30, FF4, June Bill for Fees, prisoner
   1874 Dec 23, FF3, Convicts received at the Colorado State Penitentiary from 13 June 1871 to 1 Dec 1874, Prisoner no. 2, Crime: manslaughter, County: Clear Creek, Sentence: 5 yr, Age: 35, Occupation: miner, 5 ' 8", Complexion: light, Hair: grey, Eyes: blue, Nativity: KY, Education: reads and writes

Henkle (Charles Henkle & Co)
   1876 Dec 31, FF4, Report of the Treasurer, vendor
   1877 Jan 1, FF4, Balance sheet, vendor

Herkheiser, Allen
   1874 May 29, FF4, Statement of Accounts, hardward

Hicks, J R
   1876 Dec 31, FF4, Report of the Treasurer, vendor

Hildenberg, Henry
   1872 Dec 31, FF4, Dec Bill for Fees, prisoner
   1872 July, FF4, July Bill for Fees, prisoner
   1872, Aug 31, FF4, Aug Bill for Fees, prisoner
   1873 July 31, FF4, July Bill for Fees, prisoner
   1872 May, FF4, May Bill for Fees, prisoner
   1872 May 21, FF3, Convicts dismissed from Colorado Penitentiary 13 June 1871 to 1 Dec 1874, prisoner, release no. 32, Crime: larceny, County: Arapahoe, Sentence: 1 yr 6 mo, Age: 54, discharged 1873 Aug 5, no remarks
   1873 Apr 30, FF4, April Bill for Fees, prisoner
   1873 Aug 31, FF4, Aug Bill for Fees, prisoner
   1873 June 30, FF4, June Bill for Fees, prisoner
   1873 May 31, FF4, May Bill for Fees, prisoner
   1874 Dec 23, FF3, Convicts received at the Colorado State Penitentiary from 13 June 1871 to 1 Dec 1874, Prisoner no. 39, Crime: larceny, County:

Colorado Territorial Penitentiary

Arapahoe, Sentence: 1 yr 8 mo, Age: 54, Occupation: civil engineer, 5 ' 7", Complexion: florid, Hair: grey, Eyes: blue, Nativity: Prussia, Education: no remarks

Hill, James
 1872 Dec 31, FF4, Dec Bill for Fees, prisoner
 1872 July, FF4, July Bill for Fees, prisoner
 1872 May, FF4, May Bill for Fees, prisoner
 1872, Aug 31, FF4, Aug Bill for Fees, prisoner
 1873 Apr 30, FF4, April Bill for Fees, prisoner
 1873 Aug 31, FF4, Aug Bill for Fees, prisoner
 1873 July 31, FF4, July Bill for Fees, prisoner
 1873 June 30, FF4, June Bill for Fees, prisoner
 1874 Dec 23, FF3, Convicts received at the Colorado State Penitentiary from 13 June 1871 to 1 Dec 1874, Prisoner no. 36, Crime: murder, County: Arapahoe, Sentence: life, Age: 22, 5' 4 1/2", Complexion: colored, Hair: black, Eyes: black, Nativity: AL, Education: reads and writes

Hiller, Charles
 1872 Dec 31, FF4, Dec Bill for Fees, prisoner
 1872, Aug 31, FF4, Aug Bill for Fees, prisoner

Hiller, Chas
 1872 Feb 7, FF3, Convicts dismissed from Colorado Penitentiary 13 June 1871 to 1 Dec 1874, prisoner, release no. 28, Crime: larceny, County: Arapahoe, Sentence: 1 yr, Age: 22, discharged 1872 Dec 30, no remarks
 1874 Dec 23, FF3, Convicts received at the Colorado State Penitentiary from 13 June 1871 to 1 Dec 1874, Prisoner no. 34, Crime: larceny, County: Arapahoe, Sentence: 1 yr, Age: 22, Occupation: cook, 5 ' 5 1/2", Complexion: light, Hair: very light, Eyes: lt blue, Nativity: Germany, Education: reads and writes

Hoblet, Samuel T
 1873 July 31, FF4, July Bill for Fees, prisoner

Hodges (Moynahan, Hodges & Co)
 1876 Dec 31, FF4, Report of the Treasurer, vendor

Hoover, Jacob
 1873 Apr 30, FF4, April Bill for Fees, prisoner
 1873 Aug 31, FF4, Aug Bill for Fees, prisoner
 1873 Jan 1, FF3, Convicts dismissed from Colorado Penitentiary 13 June 1871 to 1 Dec 1874, prisoner, release no. 45, Crime: larceny, County: Arapahoe, Sentence: 2 yr, Age: 29, discharged 1874 Apr 14, pardoned by Act Gov Jenkins
 1873 July 31, FF4, July Bill for Fees, prisoner
 1873 June 30, FF4, June Bill for Fees, prisoner
 1873 May 31, FF4, May Bill for Fees, prisoner
 1874 Dec 23, FF3, Convicts received at the Colorado State Penitentiary from 13 June 1871 to 1 Dec 1874, Prisoner no. 54, Crime: larceny, County: Arapahoe, Sentence: 2 yr, Age: 29, Occupation: laborer, 6 ' 1", Complexion: dark, Hair: auburn, Eyes: grey, Nativity: Baden, Education: reads and writes

Hopkins, Henry
 1874 May, FF3, Cash Accounts from the Books of A Rudd, Warden, Kansas State Penitentiary

Hopper, H
 1874 Dec 1, FF4, Balance sheet, vendor
 1875 Aug 31, FF4, Balance Sheet, vendor
 1875 Dec 6, FF4, Schedule of Open Accounts, vendor

Hopper, H C
 1874 Oct, FF3, Expenditures and Earnings of the Colorado Penitentiary, stone

Horn
 1874 May, FF3, Cash Accounts from the Books of A Rudd

Housekeeper, J C
  1874 July, FF3, Expenditures and Earnings of the Colorado Penitentiary, painting sign

Howe & Smith
  1876 Dec 31, FF4, Report of the Treasurer, vendor
  1876 Oct 13, FF4, Balance sheet, vendor

Howe Sewing Machine Co
  1875 Mar 1, FF4, Minutes of the Board of Managers, sewing machine

Hoyne (Culver, Page & Hoyne)
  1876 Dec 31, FF4, Report of the Treasurer, vendor
  1877 Jan 1, FF4, Balance sheet, vendor

Hufstaten, Chas
  1871 Dec, FF4, December Bill for Fees, prisoner
  1871 Nov, FF4, November Bill for Fees, prisoner
  1871 Oct, FF4, October Bill for Fees, prisoner

Huftalan, Chas
  1871 June 26, FF3, Convicts dismissed from Colorado Penitentiary 13 June 1871 to 1 Dec 1874, prisoner, release no. 3, Crime: burglary, County: Pueblo, Sentence: 2 yr, Age: 21, discharged 1872 May 9, sentence expired
  1874 Dec 23, FF3, Convicts received at the Colorado State Penitentiary from 13 June 1871 to 1 Dec 1874, Prisoner no. 3, Crime: burglary, County: Pueblo, Sentence: 2 yr, Age: 21, Occupation: laborer, 5 ' 10", Complexion: dark, Hair: dk brown, Eyes: grey, Nativity: NY, Education: reads and writes

Hull, W H
  1876 Oct 13, FF4, Balance sheet, vendor
  1877 Jan 1, FF4, Balance sheet, vendor

Humphrey & Co
  1874 Aug, FF3, Expenditures and Earnings of the Colorado Penitentiary, groceries
  1874 Aug 31, FF4, Minutes of the Board of Managers, vendor
  1874 Dec 1, FF4, Balance sheet, vendor
  1874 July, FF3, Expenditures and Earnings of the Colorado Penitentiary, groceries
  1874 July 21, FF3, Cash Accounts of the Colorado Penitentiary
  1874 June, FF3, Expenditures and Earnings of the Colorado Penitentiary, groceries
  1874 June, FF3, Cash Accounts from the Books of A Rudd
  1874 May, FF3, Cash Accounts from the Books of A Rudd
  1874 May, FF3, Cash Accounts from the Books of A Rudd
  1874 May 29, FF4, Statement of Accounts, provisions
  1874 May 29, FF4, Statement of Accounts, groceries
  1874 Nov, FF3, Expenditures and Earnings of the Colorado Penitentiary, groceries
  1874 Nov, FF3, Expenditures and Earnings of the Colorado Penitentiary, groceries
  1874 Sept 14, FF3, Cash Accounts of the Colorado Penitentiary
  1875 Dec 6, FF4, Schedule of Vouchers Drawn, vendor
  1875 Dec 7, FF4, Minutes of the Board of Managers, vendor
  1875 June 4, FF4, Minutes of the Board of Managers, vendor
  1875 Mar 1, FF4, Minutes of the Board of Managers, supplies
  1876 Apr 7, FF4, Balance sheet, vendor
  1876 Dec 31, FF4, Report of the Treasurer, vendor
  1876 Feb 17, FF4, Balance sheet, vendor
  1876 July 10, FF4, Balance sheet, vendor
  1876 Oct 13, FF4, Balance sheet, vendor
  1877 Jan 1, FF4, Balance sheet, vendor

Humphries & Co
  1875 Mar 1, FF4, Minutes of the Board of Managers, groceries

Colorado Territorial Penitentiary

I

Ingleman & Co
1875 Mar 1, FF4, Minutes of the Board of Managers, clothing

J

Jackson, James M
1875 Dec 6, FF4, Schedule of Vouchers Drawn, vendor

Jackson, Jas M
1875 Dec 7, FF4, Minutes of the Board of Managers, vendor

Jampson, A J
1875 Dec 6, FF4, Schedule of Open Accounts, vendor

Jans, Peter
1873 Aug 31, FF4, Aug Bill for Fees, prisoner
1874 Dec 1, FF3, Convicts Escaped since Organization of the Prison, escapee no. 13, Crime: assault to rape, County: Arapahoe, Sentence: 3 yr, Age: 29, received
1873 Aug 5, escaped 1874 Sept 19, recaptured 27 Sept 1873
1874 Dec 1, FF3, Convicts in Colorado Penitentiary on 1 Dec 1874, prisoner, Crime: assault with intent to rape, County: Arapahoe, Sentence: 3 yr, Age: 29, Occupation: cook, 5' 5"
1874 Dec 23, FF3, Convicts received at the Colorado State Penitentiary from 13 June 1871 to 1 Dec 1874, Prisoner no. 69, Crime: Assault with intent to rape, County: Arapahoe, Sentence: 3 yr, Age: 29, Occupation: cook, 5' 5", Complexion: light, Hair: light, Eyes: blue, Nativity: Germany, Education: reads and writes

Jenkins
1874 June, FF3, Cash Accounts from the Books of A Rudd, bringin in convicts

Jenkins, M J
1874 Dec 1, FF4, Balance sheet, vendor

1874 Dec 31, FF4, Expenses paid for G W Graham & Switterline, US Prisoners, bringing prisoner from Rosita
1874 July 21, FF3, Cash Accounts of the Colorado Penitentiary
1875 Jan 1, FF4, Bill for G W Graham, asst returning to prison

Jeske, Rudolph
1876 Apr 7, FF4, Balance sheet, vendor
1876 Dec 31, FF4, Report of the Treasurer, vendor
1876 Feb 17, FF4, Balance sheet, vendor
1876 July 10, FF4, Balance sheet, vendor
1876 Oct 13, FF4, Balance sheet, vendor

Joel, Lewis F
1875 Aug 31, FF4, Balance Sheet, vendor
1875 Dec 6, FF4, Schedule of Open Accounts, vendor

Johnson, Chas
1874 Dec 1, FF3, Convicts in Colorado Penitentiary on 1 Dec 1874, prisoner, Crime: larceny, County: Gilpin, Sentence: 5 yr, Age: 26, Occupation: cook, 5' 5 1/2"
1874 Dec 23, FF3, Convicts received at the Colorado State Penitentiary from 13 June 1871 to 1 Dec 1874, Prisoner no. 72, Crime: larceny, County: Gilpin, Sentence: 5 yr, Age: 26, Occupation: cook, 5' 5 1/2", Complexion: light, Hair: dk brown, Eyes: hazel, Nativity: NY, Education: reads and writes

Johnson, Ed
1871 Dec, FF4, December Bill for Fees, prisoner
1871 July 9, FF3, Convicts dismissed from Colorado Penitentiary 13 June 1871 to 1 Dec 1874, prisoner, release no. 9, Crime: larceny, County: Arapahoe, Sentence: 1 yr, Age: 22, discharged 1872 May 19, no remarks
1871 Nov, FF4, November Bill for Fees, prisoner
1871 Oct, FF4, October Bill for Fees, prisoner
1871 Oct 1, FF4, September Bill for Fees, prisoner

1872 Apr, FF4, April Bill for Fees, prisoner
1872 Jan, FF4, January Bill for Fees, prisoner
1872 May, FF4, May Bill for Fees, prisoner

Johnson, Edward
1874 Dec 23, FF3, Convicts received at the Colorado State Penitentiary from 13 June 1871 to 1 Dec 1874, Prisoner no. 9, Crime: larceny, County: Arapahoe, Sentence: 1 yr, Age: 22, Occupation: laborer, 5 ' 9 1/2", Complexion: colored, Hair: black, Eyes: black, Nativity: MD, Education: none

Johnson, Henry
1871 July 9, FF3, Convicts dismissed from Colorado Penitentiary 13 June 1871 to 1 Dec 1874, prisoner, release no. 8, Crime: larceny, County: Arapahoe, Sentence: 3 yr, Age: 24, discharged 1873 May 18, no remarks
1872 Jan, FF4, January Bill for Fees, prisoner
1872 May, FF4, May Bill for Fees, prisoner
1873 Apr 30, FF4, April Bill for Fees, prisoner
1874 Dec 23, FF3, Convicts received at the Colorado State Penitentiary from 13 June 1871 to 1 Dec 1874, Prisoner no. 8, Crime: larceny, County: Arapahoe, Sentence: 3 yr, Age: 24, Occupation: laborer, 5 ' 9", Complexion: colored, Hair: black, Eyes: black, Nativity: MD, Education: none

Johnson, Hy [Henry]
1871 Dec, FF4, December Bill for Fees, prisoner
1871 Nov, FF4, November Bill for Fees, prisoner
1871 Oct, FF4, October Bill for Fees, prisoner
1871 Oct 1, FF4, September Bill for Fees, prisoner
1872 Apr, FF4, April Bill for Fees, prisoner
1872 Dec 31, FF4, Dec Bill for Fees, prisoner
1872 July, FF4, July Bill for Fees, prisoner

1872, Aug 31, FF4, Aug Bill for Fees, prisoner
1873 May 31, FF4, May Bill for Fees, prisoner

Johnson, Jas M
1874 Dec 1, FF3, Convicts in Colorado Penitentiary on 1 Dec 1874, prisoner, Crime: forgery, County: Arapahoe, Sentence: 1 yr, Age: 21, Occupation: laborer, 1' 10 3/4"
1874 Dec 23, FF3, Convicts received at the Colorado State Penitentiary from 13 June 1871 to 1 Dec 1874, Prisoner no. 99, Crime: forgery, County: Arapahoe, Sentence: 1 yr, Age: 21, Occupation: laborer, 5 ' 10 3/4", Complexion: colored, Hair: black, Eyes: black, Nativity: KS, Education: reads and writes

Jones, Charles
1873 Aug 31, FF4, Aug Bill for Fees, prisoner
1873 July 31, FF4, July Bill for Fees, prisoner
1873 June 30, FF4, June Bill for Fees, prisoner

Jones, Chas
1874 Dec 1, FF3, Convicts in Colorado Penitentiary on 1 Dec 1874, prisoner, Crime: robbery, County: Arapahoe, Sentence: 3 yr, Age: 25, Occupation: printer, 5 ' 10"
1874 Dec 23, FF3, Convicts received at the Colorado State Penitentiary from 13 June 1871 to 1 Dec 1874, Prisoner no. 66, Crime: robbery, County: Arapahoe, Sentence: 3 yr, Age: 25, Occupation: printer, 5 ' 10", Complexion: dark, Hair: sandy, Eyes: blue, Nativity: MO, Education: reads and writes

Jones, Jackson
1873 Apr 30, FF4, April Bill for Fees, prisoner
1873 Aug 31, FF4, Aug Bill for Fees, prisoner
1873 Jan 25, FF3, Convicts dismissed from Colorado Penitentiary 13 June 1871

to 1 Dec 1874, prisoner, release no. 48, Crime: larceny, County: El Paso, Sentence: 2 yr, Age: 34, discharged 1874 Sept 29, pardoned by Act Gov Jenkins
1873 July 31, FF4, July Bill for Fees, prisoner
1873 June 30, FF4, June Bill for Fees, prisoner
1873 May 31, FF4, May Bill for Fees, prisoner
1874 Dec 23, FF3, Convicts received at the Colorado State Penitentiary from 13 June 1871 to 1 Dec 1874, Prisoner no. 57, Crime: larceny, County: El Paso, Sentence: 2 yr, Age: 34, Occupation: butcher, 5 ' 7 1/2", Complexion: dark, Hair: black, Eyes: grey, Nativity: TX, Education: reads and writes

Jones, James
1874 Apr 23, FF3, Convicts dismissed from Colorado Penitentiary 13 June 1871 to 1 Dec 1874, prisoner, release no. 58, Crime: larceny, County: Arapahoe, Sentence: 1 yr, Age: 24, discharged 1874 Oct 3, pardoned by Act Gov Jenkins
1874 Dec 23, FF3, Convicts received at the Colorado State Penitentiary from 13 June 1871 to 1 Dec 1874, Prisoner no. 81, Crime: larceny, County: Arapahoe, Sentence: 1 yr, Age: 24, Occupation: laborer, 5 ' 9 1/2", Complexion: colored, Hair: black, Eyes: black, Nativity: MS, Education: reads only

K

Kansas State Penitentiary
1874 May 29, FF4, Statement of Accounts, clothing

Kelly, William
1873 Apr 30, FF4, April Bill for Fees, prisoner
1873 Aug 31, FF4, Aug Bill for Fees, prisoner
1873 July 31, FF4, July Bill for Fees, prisoner
1873 June 30, FF4, June Bill for Fees, prisoner
1873 May 31, FF4, May Bill for Fees, prisoner

Kelly, Wm
1873 Jan 25, FF3, Convicts dismissed from Colorado Penitentiary 13 June 1871 to 1 Dec 1874, prisoner, release no. 47, Crime: larceny, County: El Paso, Sentence: 1 yr 6 mo, Age: 23, discharged 1874 May 10, no remarks
1874 Dec 23, FF3, Convicts received at the Colorado State Penitentiary from 13 June 1871 to 1 Dec 1874, Prisoner no. 56, Crime: larceny, County: El Paso, Sentence: 1 yr 8 mo, Age: 23, Occupation: sailor, 5 ' 5 1/4", Complexion: dark, Hair: black, Eyes: grey, Nativity: Ireland, Education: reads and writes

Kemp, Tully
1875 Dec 6, FF4, Schedule of Vouchers Drawn, vendor
1875 Dec 7, FF4, Minutes of the Board of Managers, vendor

Kennedy (Mack & Kennedy)
1876 Apr 7, FF4, Balance sheet, vendor
1876 Dec 31, FF4, Report of the Treasurer, vendor
1876 Feb 17, FF4, Balance sheet, vendor
1876 July 10, FF4, Balance sheet, vendor
1876 Oct 13, FF4, Balance sheet, vendor
1877 Jan 1, FF4, Balance sheet, vendor

Kimbrough
1874 June, FF3, Cash Accounts from the Books of A Rudd, wood

Knight, George
1872 Dec 31, FF4, Dec Bill for Fees, prisoner
1872 July, FF4, July Bill for Fees, prisoner
1872 June 18, FF3, Convicts dismissed from Colorado Penitentiary 13 June 1871 to 1 Dec 1874, prisoner, release no. 37, Crime: larceny, County: Pueblo, Sentence: 3 yr, Age: 31, discharged 1874 June 30, pardoned by Act Gov Jenkins
1872, Aug 31, FF4, Aug Bill for Fees, prisoner

1873 Apr 30, FF4, April Bill for Fees, prisoner
1873 Aug 31, FF4, Aug Bill for Fees, prisoner
1873 July 31, FF4, July Bill for Fees, prisoner
1873 June 30, FF4, June Bill for Fees, prisoner
1873 May 31, FF4, May Bill for Fees, prisoner
1874 Dec 23, FF3, Convicts received at the Colorado State Penitentiary from 13 June 1871 to 1 Dec 1874, Prisoner no. 45, Crime: larceny, County: Pueblo, Sentence: 3 yr, Age: 31, Occupation: blacksmith, 5 ' 7 1/2", Complexion: medium, Hair: brown, Eyes: blue, Nativity: MA, Education: reads and writes

Kraft, J M
1875 Dec 7, FF4, Minutes of the Board of Managers, vendor

Kraft, J W
1875 Dec 6, FF4, Schedule of Vouchers Drawn, vendor
1876 Apr 7, FF4, Balance sheet, vendor
1876 Dec 31, FF4, Report of the Treasurer, vendor
1876 Feb 17, FF4, Balance sheet, vendor
1876 July 10, FF4, Balance sheet, vendor
1876 Oct 13, FF4, Balance sheet, vendor

L

Lamb, Joseph
1874 May, FF3, Cash Accounts from the Books of A Rudd
1874 May 29, FF4, Statement of Accounts, lumber

Lambert & Co
1876 Apr 7, FF4, Balance sheet, vendor
1876 Dec 31, FF4, Report of the Treasurer, vendor
1876 Oct 13, FF4, Balance sheet, vendor

Lambert, J J
1877 Apr 11, FF4, Balance sheet, vendor

Ledges (Moynahan & Ledges & Co)
1876 Apr 7, FF4, Balance sheet, vendor

Leslie, William W
1872 Dec 31, FF4, Dec Bill for Fees, prisoner
1872, Aug 31, FF4, Aug Bill for Fees, prisoner

Leslie, Wm W
1872 June 18, FF3, Convicts dismissed from Colorado Penitentiary 13 June 1871 to 1 Dec 1874, prisoner, release no. 36, Crime: larceny, County: Pueblo, Sentence: 1 yr, Age: 24, discharged 1873 Jan 22, pardoned by ____
1874 Dec 23, FF3, Convicts received at the Colorado State Penitentiary from 13 June 1871 to 1 Dec 1874, Prisoner no. 44, Crime: larceny, County: Pueblo, Sentence: 1 ur, Age: 24, Occupation: laborer, 5 ' 7 1/4", Complexion: fair, Hair: dk brown, Eyes: blue grey, Nativity: WI, Education: reads and writes

Lewis, A C
1871 Dec, FF4, December Bill for Fees, prisoner
1871 Nov, FF4, November Bill for Fees, prisoner
1872 May, FF4, May Bill for Fees, prisoner
1875 Dec 7, FF4, Minutes of the Board of Managers, vendor

Lewis, George
1872 Dec 31, FF4, Dec Bill for Fees, prisoner
1872 July, FF4, July Bill for Fees, prisoner
1872 June 18, FF3, Convicts dismissed from Colorado Penitentiary 13 June 1871 to 1 Dec 1874, prisoner, release no. 38, Crime: larceny, County: Pueblo, Sentence: 1 yr, Age: 23, discharged 1873 May 10, no remarks
1872, Aug 31, FF4, Aug Bill for Fees, prisoner
1873 Apr 30, FF4, April Bill for Fees, prisoner
1873 May 31, FF4, May Bill for Fees, prisoner

Colorado Territorial Penitentiary

1874 Dec 23, FF3, Convicts received at the Colorado State Penitentiary from 13 June 1871 to 1 Dec 1874, Prisoner no. 47, Crime: larceny, County: Pueblo, Sentence: 1 yr, Age: 23, Occupation: barber, 5' 8", Complexion: colored, Hair: black, Eyes: black, Nativity: OH, Education: reads and writes

Lewis, I F
1875 Dec 6, FF4, Schedule of Vouchers Drawn, vendor

Lewis, L A
1876 Dec 31, FF4, Report of the Treasurer, vendor
1876 Feb 17, FF4, Balance sheet, vendor

Lime Kiln
1874 Nov, FF3, Table showing days worked, 6 4

Lisbin, William W
1872 July, FF4, July Bill for Fees, prisoner

Lobenstein Ruble & Co
1874 Dec 1, FF4, Minutes of the Board of Managers, leather & tools

Lobenstein Ruble & Co
1874 Dec 1, FF4, Balance sheet, vendor
1874 Oct, FF3, Expenditures and Earnings of the Colorado Penitentiary, leather
1874 Sept, FF3, Expenditures and Earnings of the Colorado Penitentiary, leather
1875 Dec 6, FF4, Schedule of Vouchers Drawn, vendor
1875 Dec 7, FF4, Minutes of the Board of Managers, vendor
1875 June 4, FF4, Minutes of the Board of Managers, vendor
1875 Mar 1, FF4, Minutes of the Board of Managers, leather
1876 Apr 7, FF4, Balance sheet, vendor
1876 Dec 31, FF4, Report of the Treasurer, vendor

Locke
1874 May, FF3, Convict Labor Administered by Anson Rudd, 7 1/2 days

Locke (Adams & Locke)
1874 Nov, FF3, Expenditures and Earnings of the Colorado Penitentiary, stone

Locke, Adam
1874 Dec 1, FF4, Balance sheet, vendor

Logan, I L
1876 Oct 13, FF4, Balance sheet, vendor

Logan, J L
1876 Apr 7, FF4, Balance sheet, vendor

Logan, J S
1876 Dec 31, FF4, Report of the Treasurer, vendor

Londoner & Bro
1874 Aug, FF3, Expenditures and Earnings of the Colorado Penitentiary, groceries
1874 Aug 31, FF4, Minutes of the Board of Managers, vendor
1874 Dec 1, FF4, Minutes of the Board of Managers, groceries
1874 July, FF3, Expenditures and Earnings of the Colorado Penitentiary, groceries
1874 Oct, FF3, Expenditures and Earnings of the Colorado Penitentiary, groceries
1874 Sept, FF3, Expenditures and Earnings of the Colorado Penitentiary, groceries
1874 Sept 10, FF3, Cash Accounts of the Colorado Penitentiary
1875 Aug 31, FF4, Balance Sheet, vendor
1875 Dec 7, FF4, Minutes of the Board of Managers, vendor
1875 Mar 1, FF4, Minutes of the Board of Managers, groceries
1875 Mar 1, FF4, Minutes of the Board of Managers, groceries
1876 Dec 31, FF4, Report of the Treasurer, vendor

Londoner & Bros
1875 June 4, FF4, Minutes of the Board of Managers, vendor

Londoner Bro
1875 Aug 31, FF4, Schedule of Vouchers Drawn, vendor

Londoner Bros
1874 Dec 1, FF4, Balance sheet, vendor

Board of Managers Reports, 1871-1877

1875 Dec 6, FF4, Schedule of Vouchers Drawn, vendor
1876 Apr 7, FF4, Balance sheet, vendor
1876 July 10, FF4, Balance sheet, vendor
1876 Oct 13, FF4, Balance sheet, vendor

Lottas, Fred
1873 Jan 1, FF3, Convicts dismissed from Colorado Penitentiary 13 June 1871 to 1 Dec 1874, prisoner, release no. 43, Crime: manslaughter, County: Lake, Sentence: 2 yr, Age: 35, discharged 1874 Sept 14, pardoned by Gov McCook
1874 Dec 23, FF3, Convicts received at the Colorado State Penitentiary from 13 June 1871 to 1 Dec 1874, Prisoner no. 52, Crime: manslaughter, County: Lake, Sentence: 2 yr, Age: 35, Occupation: miner, 5 ' 9 1/2", Complexion: dark, Hair: auburn, Eyes: grey, Nativity: Bavaria, Education: reads and writes

Lottes, Frederick
1873 Apr 30, FF4, April Bill for Fees, prisoner
1873 Aug 31, FF4, Aug Bill for Fees, prisoner
1873 July 31, FF4, July Bill for Fees, prisoner
1873 June 30, FF4, June Bill for Fees, prisoner
1873 May 31, FF4, May Bill for Fees, prisoner

Lyar, Abraham
1873 Aug 31, FF4, Aug Bill for Fees, prisoner

Lysle, Abraham
1873 ug 5, FF3, Convicts dismissed from Colorado Penitentiary 13 June 1871 to 1 Dec 1874, prisoner, release no. 53, Crime: larceny, County: Arapahoe, Sentence: 1 yr, Age: 22, discharged 1874 May 28, no remarks
1874 Dec 23, FF3, Convicts received at the Colorado State Penitentiary from 13 June 1871 to 1 Dec 1874, Prisoner no. 68, Crime: larceny, County: Arapahoe, Sentence: 1 yr, Age: 22, Occupation: laborer, 5 ' 9", Complexion: colored, Hair: black, Eyes: black, Nativity: MO, Education: reads and writes

M

Mack & Kennedy
1876 Apr 7, FF4, Balance sheet, vendor
1876 Dec 31, FF4, Report of the Treasurer, vendor
1876 Feb 17, FF4, Balance sheet, vendor
1876 July 10, FF4, Balance sheet, vendor
1876 Oct 13, FF4, Balance sheet, vendor
1877 Jan 1, FF4, Balance sheet, vendor

Mack & Magee
1877 Jan 1, FF4, Balance sheet, vendor

Mack (McGee & Mack)
1876 Dec 31, FF4, Report of the Treasurer, vendor
1876 July 10, FF4, Balance sheet, vendor
1877 Apr 11, FF4, Balance sheet, vendor

Mackey, Richard
1873 Oct 25, FF3, Convicts dismissed from Colorado Penitentiary 13 June 1871 to 1 Dec 1874, prisoner, release no. 55, Crime: murder, County: Gilpin, Sentence: 1 yr 6 mo, Age: 27, discharged 1874 May 5, pardoned by Act Gov Jenkins
1874 Dec 23, FF3, Convicts received at the Colorado State Penitentiary from 13 June 1871 to 1 Dec 1874, Prisoner no. 73, Crime: murder, County: Gilpin, Sentence: 1 yr 6 mo, Age: 27, Occupation: miner, 5 ' 7", Complexion: dark, Hair: dark, Eyes: grey, Nativity: Ireland, Education: reads and writes

Macon, Thomas
1874 Nov 13, FF3, Cash Accounts of the Colorado Penitentiary
1875 Aug 31, FF4, Balance Sheet, vendor
1875 Dec 6, FF4, Schedule of Open Accounts, vendor

Macon, Thos
1874 Dec 1, FF4, Balance sheet, vendor
1874 July, FF3, Expenditures and Earnings of the Colorado Penitentiary, painting buggy

Colorado Territorial Penitentiary

Magee (Mack & Magee)
1877 Jan 1, FF4, Balance sheet, vendor

Manzanares, M A
1872 Jan, FF4, January Bill for Fees, prisoner
1873 June 30, FF4, June Bill for Fees, prisoner
1873 May 31, FF4, May Bill for Fees, prisoner

Manzanares, Maria A
1872 Apr, FF4, April Bill for Fees, prisoner
1872 Dec 31, FF4, Dec Bill for Fees, prisoner
1872 Jan 3, FF3, Convicts dismissed from Colorado Penitentiary 13 June 1871 to 1 Dec 1874, prisoner, release no. 20, Crime: murder, County: Pueblo, Sentence: life, Age: 26, discharged, no record, pardoned by ____
1872 July, FF4, July Bill for Fees, prisoner
1872 May, FF4, May Bill for Fees, prisoner
1872, Aug 31, FF4, Aug Bill for Fees, prisoner
1873 Apr 30, FF4, April Bill for Fees, prisoner
1873 Aug 31, FF4, Aug Bill for Fees, prisoner
1873 July 31, FF4, July Bill for Fees, prisoner
1874 Dec 23, FF3, Convicts received at the Colorado State Penitentiary from 13 June 1871 to 1 Dec 1874, Prisoner no. 24, Crime: murder, County: Pueblo, Sentence: life, Age: 26, 5' 3", Complexion: yellow, Hair: black, Eyes: black, Nativity: NM, Education: none

Marley, J Q
1874 May 29, FF4, Statement of Accounts, Auditor

Mason, Thomas
1874 Dec 1, FF3, Convicts Escaped since Organization of the Prison, escapee no. 16, Crime: larceny, County: Arapahoe, Sentence: 3 yr, Age: 30, received 1874 Jan 9, escaped 1874 May 26, recaptured 10 June 1874
1874 Dec 23, FF3, Convicts received at the Colorado State Penitentiary from 13 June 1871 to 1 Dec 1874, Prisoner no. 76, Crime: larceny, County: Arapahoe, Sentence: 3 yr, Age: 30, Occupation: laborer, 5 ' 10", Complexion: dark, Hair: sandy, Eyes: grey, Nativity: NY, Education: reads and writes

Mason, Thos
1874 Dec 1, FF3, Convicts in Colorado Penitentiary on 1 Dec 1874, prisoner, Crime: larceny, County: Arapahoe, Sentence: 3 yr, Age: 30, Occupation: laborer, 5 ' 10"

Mayall (John Mayall & Co)
1875 June 4, FF4, Minutes of the Board of Managers, vendor
1875 Mar 1, FF4, Minutes of the Board of Managers, ticking, muslin

McClure
1874 June, FF3, Cash Accounts from the Books of A Rudd, eggs
1874 June, FF3, Cash Accounts from the Books of A Rudd, merchandise

McClure, J
1874 Nov, FF3, Expenditures and Earnings of the Colorado Penitentiary, groceries

McClure, John
1874 Nov, FF3, Expenditures and Earnings of the Colorado Penitentiary, cut stone
1874 Nov 3, FF3, Cash Accounts of the Colorado Penitentiary

McClure, John C
1874 Dec 1, FF4, Balance sheet, vendor
1874 May 29, FF4, Statement of Accounts, wood
1875 Aug 31, FF4, Balance Sheet, vendor

McClure, W H
1876 Dec 31, FF4, Report of the Treasurer, vendor
1877 Jan 1, FF4, Balance sheet, vendor

McClure, Wm H
1876 Apr 7, FF4, Balance sheet, vendor
1876 Dec 31, FF4, Report of the Treasurer, vendor
1876 July 10, FF4, Balance sheet, vendor

Board of Managers Reports, 1871-1877

McCook, Edwin M
1871 Dec 2, FF4, Auditor's Letter, Commissioner
1871 Dec 31, FF4, Auditor's Letter, Commissioner
1871 Nov 7, FF4, Auditor's Letter, Commissioner
1871 Oct 5, FF4, Auditor's Letter, Commissioner

McCoy, Nathan
1874 Dec 1, FF3, Convicts in Colorado Penitentiary on 1 Dec 1874, prisoner, Crime: burglary, County: Arapahoe, Sentence: 2 yr, Age: 22, Occupation: laborer, 5 ' 11"
1874 Dec 23, FF3, Convicts received at the Colorado State Penitentiary from 13 June 1871 to 1 Dec 1874, Prisoner no. 95, Crime: burglary, County: Arapahoe, Sentence: 2 yr, Age: 22, Occupation: laborer, 5 ' 11", Complexion: colored, Hair: black, Eyes: black, Nativity: KY, Education: none

McCune, Jno
1875 Mar 1, FF4, Minutes of the Board of Managers, Guard

McCune, John
1874 Dec 1, FF3, Convicts in Colorado Penitentiary on 1 Dec 1874, prisoner, Crime: larceny, County: Gilpin, Sentence: 1 yr 6 mo, Age: 36, Occupation: laborer, 5 ' 7"
1874 Dec 23, FF3, Convicts received at the Colorado State Penitentiary from 13 June 1871 to 1 Dec 1874, Prisoner no. 87, Crime: larceny, County: Gilpin, Sentence: 1 yr 6 mo, Age: 36, Occupation: laborer, 5 ' 7", Complexion: light, Hair: dark, Eyes: blue, Nativity: Ireland, Education: none

McDonald, Jno R
1874 Dec 1, FF3, Convicts in Colorado Penitentiary on 1 Dec 1874, prisoner, Crime: assault to rob, County: Las Animas, Sentence: 5 yr, Age: 27, Occupation: sadler, 5 ' 7"

McDonald, John R
1874 Dec 23, FF3, Convicts received at the Colorado State Penitentiary from 13 June 1871 to 1 Dec 1874, Prisoner no. 94, Crime: assault with intent to rob, County: Las Animas, Sentence: 5 yr, Age: 27, Occupation: saddler, 5 ' 7", Complexion: light, Hair: dark, Eyes: grey, Nativity: TN, Education: reads and writes

McGee & Mace
1875 June 4, FF4, Minutes of the Board of Managers, vendor

McGee & Mack
1876 Dec 31, FF4, Report of the Treasurer, vendor
1876 July 10, FF4, Balance sheet, vendor
1877 Apr 11, FF4, Balance sheet, vendor

McGrace Mach
1875 Aug 31, FF4, Balance Sheet, vendor

McGrew (Bain & McGrew)
1876 Dec 31, FF4, Report of the Treasurer, vendor
1876 July 10, FF4, Balance sheet, vendor
1876 Oct 13, FF4, Balance sheet, vendor
1877 Jan 1, FF4, Balance sheet, vendor

McKay, Chas E
1876 Dec 31, FF4, Report of the Treasurer, vendor

McKnight, James
1876 Apr 7, FF4, Balance sheet, vendor
1876 Dec 31, FF4, Report of the Treasurer, vendor

McMahan, John
1872 Jan 10, FF3, Convicts dismissed from Colorado Penitentiary 13 June 1871 to 1 Dec 1874, prisoner, release no. 24, Crime: attempt to murder, County: Boulder, Sentence: 1 yr, Age: 38, discharged 1872 Dec 5, no remarks
1874 Dec 23, FF3, Convicts received at the Colorado State Penitentiary from 13 June 1871 to 1 Dec 1874, Prisoner no. 30, Crime: assault with intent to commit murder, County: Boulder, Sentence: 1 yr, Age: 38, Occupation:

Colorado Territorial Penitentiary

miner, 5 ' 8", Complexion: florid, Hair: grey, Eyes: blue, Nativity: Ireland, Education: reads and writes
1872 Apr, FF4, April Bill for Fees, prisoner
1872 Dec 31, FF4, Dec Bill for Fees, prisoner
1872 Jan, FF4, January Bill for Fees, prisoner
1872 July, FF4, July Bill for Fees, prisoner
1872 May, FF4, May Bill for Fees, prisoner
1872, Aug 31, FF4, Aug Bill for Fees, prisoner

McRay, C E
1877 Apr 11, FF4, Balance sheet, vendor

McRay, Chas E
1876 Apr 7, FF4, Balance sheet, vendor
1876 Dec 31, FF4, Report of the Treasurer, vendor
1876 Feb 17, FF4, Balance sheet, vendor
1876 July 10, FF4, Balance sheet, vendor

McRay, I E
1876 Oct 13, FF4, Balance sheet, vendor
1877 Apr 11, FF4, Balance sheet, vendor
1877 Jan 1, FF4, Balance sheet, vendor

McRay, J E
1876 Dec 31, FF4, Report of the Treasurer, vendor

Meckheiser (Allen & Meckheiser)
1874 Dec 1, FF4, Minutes of the Board of Managers, hardware

Merritt, J H
1874 July, FF3, Expenditures and Earnings of the Colorado Penitentiary, 1 day labor
1874 July, FF3, Table showing days worked, 1
1874 July 21, FF3, Cash Accounts of the Colorado Penitentiary
1875 Dec 6, FF4, Schedule of Vouchers Drawn, vendor
1875 Dec 7, FF4, Minutes of the Board of Managers, vendor
1875 Mar 1, FF4, Minutes of the Board of Managers, Chaplain
1876 Apr 7, FF4, Balance sheet, vendor
1876 Dec 31, FF4, Report of the Treasurer, vendor
1876 Dec 31, FF4, Report of the Treasurer, vendor
1876 Feb 17, FF4, Balance sheet, vendor
1876 July 10, FF4, Balance sheet, vendor

Merritt, Rev J H
1876 Dec 31, FF4, Report of the Treasurer, vendor

Meyer, Charles
1872, Aug 31, FF4, Aug Bill for Fees, prisoner

Midmore, Y B
1874 Dec 1, FF4, Balance sheet, vendor

Miller, Chas
1871 Nov, FF4, November Bill for Fees, prisoner

Mills, Charles
1872 July, FF4, July Bill for Fees, prisoner

Millsap, George
1874 Dec 1, FF3, Convicts Escaped since Organization of the Prison, escapee no. 11, Crime: robbery, County: Arapahoe, Sentence: 3 yr, Age: 23, received 1873 June 25, escaped 1874 May 26, recaptured 10 June 1874
1874 Dec 1, FF3, Convicts in Colorado Penitentiary on 1 Dec 1874, prisoner, Crime: robbery, County: Arapahoe, Sentence: 3 yr, Age: 23, Occupation: laborer, 5 ' 10"
1874 Dec 23, FF3, Convicts received at the Colorado State Penitentiary from 13 June 1871 to 1 Dec 1874, Prisoner no. 65, Crime: robbery, County: Arapahoe, Sentence: 3 yr, Age: 23, Occupation: laborer, 5 ' 10", Complexion: light, Hair: dark, Eyes: hazel, Nativity: VA, Education: reads and writes
1873 Aug 31, FF4, Aug Bill for Fees, prisoner
1873 July 31, FF4, July Bill for Fees, prisoner
1873 June 30, FF4, June Bill for Fees, prisoner

Mitchell, Charles W
1872 Dec 31, FF4, Dec Bill for Fees, prisoner

1872 July, FF4, July Bill for Fees, prisoner
1872, Aug 31, FF4, Aug Bill for Fees, prisoner
1873 Apr 30, FF4, April Bill for Fees, prisoner
1873 Aug 31, FF4, Aug Bill for Fees, prisoner
1873 July 31, FF4, July Bill for Fees, prisoner
1873 June 30, FF4, June Bill for Fees, prisoner
1873 May 31, FF4, May Bill for Fees, prisoner

Mitchell, Chas W
1872 June 18, FF3, Convicts dismissed from Colorado Penitentiary 13 June 1871 to 1 Dec 1874, prisoner, release no. 34, Crime: larceny, County: Pueblo, Sentence: 2 yr, Age: 36, discharged 1873 June 13, no remarks
1874 Dec 23, FF3, Convicts received at the Colorado State Penitentiary from 13 June 1871 to 1 Dec 1874, Prisoner no. 42, Crime: larceny, County: Pueblo, Sentence: 2 yr, Age: 36, Occupation: farmer, 5 ' 11 1/2", Complexion: dark, Hair: black, Eyes: brown, Nativity: VA, Education: none

Morris (Saeton & Morris)
1875 Mar 1, FF4, Minutes of the Board of Managers, horse hire
1874 Nov, FF3, Expenditures and Earnings of the Colorado Penitentiary, horse hire and draying

Morrison, Robert
1875 Aug 31, FF4, Balance Sheet, vendor
1875 Dec 6, FF4, Schedule of Open Accounts, vendor

Moynahan & Ledges & Co
1876 Apr 7, FF4, Balance sheet, vendor

Moynahan, Hodges & Co
1876 Dec 31, FF4, Report of the Treasurer, vendor

Mullen, John
1874 Dec 1, FF3, Convicts in Colorado Penitentiary on 1 Dec 1874, prisoner, Crime: larceny, County: Bent, Sentence: 2 yr, Age: 19, Occupation: laborer, 5 ' 9"

Mullen, John
1874 Dec 23, FF3, Convicts received at the Colorado State Penitentiary from 13 June 1871 to 1 Dec 1874, Prisoner no. 92, Crime: larceny, County: Bent, Sentence: 2 yr, Age: 19, Occupation: laborer, 5 ' 9", Complexion: dark, Hair: dark, Eyes: black, Nativity: NY, Education: reads and writes

Myrick
1877 Apr 11, FF4, Balance sheet, vendor

N

Noblet, Samuel T
1873 Apr 30, FF4, April Bill for Fees, prisoner
1873 Aug 31, FF4, Aug Bill for Fees, prisoner
1873 June 30, FF4, June Bill for Fees, prisoner
1873 May 31, FF4, May Bill for Fees, prisoner

Noblett, Saml T
1874 Dec 1, FF3, Convicts in Colorado Penitentiary on 1 Dec 1874, prisoner, Crime: larceny and burglary, County: Boulder, Sentence: 5 yr, Age: 55, Occupation: carpenter, 5 ' 5"
1874 Dec 23, FF3, Convicts received at the Colorado State Penitentiary from 13 June 1871 to 1 Dec 1874, Prisoner no. 59, Crime: larceny and burglary, County: Boulder, Sentence: 5 yr, Age: 55, Occupation: carpenter, 5 ' 5", Complexion: light, Hair: sandy, Eyes: grey, Nativity: PA, Education: reads and writes

O

O'Boyle, P C
1873 July 31, FF4, July Bill for Fees, prisoner

Colorado Territorial Penitentiary

O'Boyle, Patrick C
  1873 Aug 31, FF4, Aug Bill for Fees, prisoner
  1873 June 30, FF4, June Bill for Fees, prisoner
  1873 May 31, FF4, May Bill for Fees, prisoner

O'Boyle, Wm C
  1873 Apr 27, FF3, Convicts dismissed from Colorado Penitentiary 13 June 1871 to 1 Dec 1874, prisoner, release no. 51, Crime: salting mines, County: Clear Creek, Sentence: 1 yr, Age: 31, discharged 1874 Apr 7, pardoned by Act Gov Jenkins
  1874 Dec 23, FF3, Convicts received at the Colorado State Penitentiary from 13 June 1871 to 1 Dec 1874, Prisoner no. 61, Crime: salting mines, County: Clear Creek, Sentence: 1 yr, Age: 31, Occupation: machinist, 5 ' 10 1/2", Complexion: dark, Hair: black, Eyes: hazel, Nativity: Ireland, Education: reads and writes

Oliver, Wm
  1874 Dec 1, FF3, Convicts in Colorado Penitentiary on 1 Dec 1874, prisoner, Crime: assault to kill, County: Bent, Sentence: 10 yr, Age: 27, Occupation: laborer, 5 ' 7"
  1874 Dec 23, FF3, Convicts received at the Colorado State Penitentiary from 13 June 1871 to 1 Dec 1874, Prisoner no. 90, Crime: assault with intent to kill, County: Bent, Sentence: 10 yr, Age: 27, Occupation: laborer, 5 ' 7", Complexion: light, Hair: dark, Eyes: blue, Nativity: Canada, Education: reads and writes

P

Packard, E O
  1874 July 21, FF3, Cash Accounts of the Colorado Penitentiary

Packard, Elroy
  1874 Aug 31, FF4, Minutes of the Board of Managers, vendor

Page (Culver, Page & Hoyne)
  1876 Dec 31, FF4, Report of the Treasurer, vendor
  1877 Jan 1, FF4, Balance sheet, vendor

Patterson, Norman
  1872 Dec 16, FF3, Convicts dismissed from Colorado Penitentiary 13 June 1871 to 1 Dec 1874, prisoner, release no. 41, Crime: murder, County: Pueblo, Sentence: 2 yr, Age: 20, discharged 1874 Sept 29, pardoned by Act Gov Jenkins
  1873 Apr 30, FF4, April Bill for Fees, prisoner
  1873 Aug 31, FF4, Aug Bill for Fees, prisoner
  1873 July 31, FF4, July Bill for Fees, prisoner
  1873 June 30, FF4, June Bill for Fees, prisoner
  1873 May 31, FF4, May Bill for Fees, prisoner
  1874 Dec 23, FF3, Convicts received at the Colorado State Penitentiary from 13 June 1871 to 1 Dec 1874, Prisoner no. 50, Crime: murder, County: Pueblo, Sentence: 2 yr, Age: 20, Occupation: farmer, 5 ' 10 1/2", Complexion: light, Hair: dark, Eyes: hazel, Nativity: MO, Education: reads and writes

Pattison, L W
  1876 Apr 7, FF4, Balance sheet, vendor
  1876 Dec 31, FF4, Report of the Treasurer, vendor
  1876 Feb 17, FF4, Balance sheet, vendor
  1876 July 10, FF4, Balance sheet, vendor

Payne, R C
  1874 Dec 1, FF3, Convicts in Colorado Penitentiary on 1 Dec 1874, prisoner, Crime: larceny, County: Pueblo, Sentence: 2 yr, Age: 39, Occupation: miner, 5 ' 10 3/4"
  1874 Dec 23, FF3, Convicts received at the Colorado State Penitentiary from 13 June 1871 to 1 Dec 1874, Prisoner no. 93, Crime: larceny, County: Pueblo, Sentence: 2 yr, Age: 39, Occupation: miner, 5 10 3/4", Complexion: florid,

Hair: light, Eyes: blue, Nativity: NY, Education: reads and writes

Peabody, D G
1875 Dec 6, FF4, Schedule of Vouchers Drawn, vendor
1875 Dec 7, FF4, Minutes of the Board of Managers, vendor
1875 June 4, FF4, Minutes of the Board of Managers, vendor
1876 Apr 7, FF4, Balance sheet, vendor
1876 Dec 31, FF4, Report of the Treasurer, vendor

Pearsen, D
1875 Mar 1, FF4, Minutes of the Board of Managers, Warden

Pearsen, D A
1875 Mar 1, FF4, Minutes of the Board of Managers, Turnkey

Perry, Charles L
1872 Dec 31, FF4, Dec Bill for Fees, prisoner
1872 July, FF4, July Bill for Fees, prisoner
1872, Aug 31, FF4, Aug Bill for Fees, prisoner

Perry, Chas L
1874 Dec 1, FF3, Convicts Escaped since Organization of the Prison, escapee no. 8, Crime: larceny, County: Pueblo, Sentence: 1 yr, Age: 29, received 1872 June 18, escaped 1873 Jan 18, still at large
1874 Dec 23, FF3, Convicts received at the Colorado State Penitentiary from 13 June 1871 to 1 Dec 1874, Prisoner no. 46, Crime: larceny, County: Pueblo, Sentence: 1 yr, Age: 29, Occupation: carpenter, 5 ' 10 1/2", Complexion: medium, Hair: brown, Eyes: blue, Nativity: MA, Education: reads and writes

Philips, Geo
1874 Dec 1, FF4, Minutes of the Board of Managers, beef

Phillips, G T
1876 Dec 31, FF4, Report of the Treasurer, vendor

Phillips, Geo
1874 Aug, FF3, Expenditures and Earnings of the Colorado Penitentiary, meat
1874 Aug 31, FF4, Minutes of the Board of Managers, vendor
1874 July, FF3, Expenditures and Earnings of the Colorado Penitentiary, meat
1874 June, FF3, Cash Accounts from the Books of A Rudd
1874 June, FF3, Expenditures and Earnings of the Colorado Penitentiary, meat
1874 May, FF3, Cash Accounts from the Books of A Rudd
1874 May 29, FF4, Statement of Accounts, beef
1874 Nov, FF3, Expenditures and Earnings of the Colorado Penitentiary, meat
1874 Sept 14, FF3, Cash Accounts of the Colorado Penitentiary
1874 Sept 30, FF3, Cash Accounts of the Colorado Penitentiary
1877 Apr 11, FF4, Balance sheet, vendor

Phillips, Geo T
1874 Dec 1, FF4, Balance sheet, vendor
1875 Aug 31, FF4, Balance Sheet, vendor
1875 Dec 6, FF4, Schedule of Vouchers Drawn, vendor
1875 Dec 7, FF4, Minutes of the Board of Managers, vendor
1875 June 4, FF4, Minutes of the Board of Managers, vendor
1875 Mar 1, FF4, Minutes of the Board of Managers, beef
1876 Apr 7, FF4, Balance sheet, vendor
1876 Dec 31, FF4, Report of the Treasurer, vendor
1876 Feb 17, FF4, Balance sheet, vendor
1876 July 10, FF4, Balance sheet, vendor
1876 Oct 13, FF4, Balance sheet, vendor

Phillips, Y T
1877 Jan 1, FF4, Balance sheet, vendor

Platt (Quinn & Platt)
1875 Aug 31, FF4, Balance Sheet, vendor

Colorado Territorial Penitentiary

Prentice, J L
1875 Mar 1, FF4, Minutes of the Board of Managers, drugs

Prentiss
1874 Nov, FF3, Expenditures and Earnings of the Colorado Penitentiary, medicines

Prentiss & Harrison
1874 Dec 1, FF4, Balance sheet, vendor
1875 Aug 31, FF4, Balance Sheet, vendor
1875 Dec 6, FF4, Schedule of Open Accounts, vendor

Prentiss, Dr
1874 Dec 31, FF4, Expenses paid for G W Graham & Switterline, US Prisoners, Doctor at Canon City
1875 Dec 7, FF4, Minutes of the Board of Managers, vendor

Prentiss, Dr J L
1876 Dec 31, FF4, Report of the Treasurer, vendor

Prentiss, J L
1874 Aug, FF3, Expenditures and Earnings of the Colorado Penitentiary, medicines
1874 Aug 31, FF4, Minutes of the Board of Managers, vendor
1874 Dec 1, FF4, Balance sheet, vendor
1874 July, FF3, Expenditures and Earnings of the Colorado Penitentiary, medicines
1874 July, FF3, Expenditures and Earnings of the Colorado Penitentiary, painting buggy
1874 July, FF3, Table showing days worked, 3.5
1874 June, FF3, Expenditures and Earnings of the Colorado Penitentiary, medicines
1874 June, FF3, Cash Accounts from the Books of A Rudd
1874 May, FF3, Cash Accounts from the Books of A Rudd
1874 May 29, FF4, Statement of Accounts, oil, medicine & prof services
1874 May 29, FF4, Statement of Accounts, coal oil, musician, prof services
1874 Sept 14, FF3, Cash Accounts of the Colorado Penitentiary
1875 Aug 31, FF4, Balance Sheet, vendor
1875 Dec 6, FF4, Schedule of Vouchers Drawn, vendor
1875 June 4, FF4, Minutes of the Board of Managers, vendor
1875 Mar 1, FF4, Minutes of the Board of Managers, drugs & attendance
1876 Apr 7, FF4, Balance sheet, vendor
1876 Dec 31, FF4, Report of the Treasurer, vendor
1876 July 10, FF4, Balance sheet, vendor
1876 Oct 13, FF4, Balance sheet, vendor
1877 Apr 11, FF4, Balance sheet, vendor
1877 Jan 1, FF4, Balance sheet, vendor
1876 Feb 17, FF4, Balance sheet, vendor

Pringle, James
1875 Mar 3, FF4, Minutes of the Board of Managers, officer

Prison Roof
1874 Nov, FF3, Table showing days worked, 12.5

Prosser, D
1874 Oct 24, FF3, Cash accounts
1875 Jan 1, FF4, Bill for G W Graham, expenses to Rosita

Prosser, David
1874 Aug 18, FF3, Cash Accounts of the Colorado Penitentiary
1874 Aug 31, FF4, Minutes of the Board of Managers, vendor
1874 Dec 1, FF4, Minutes of the Board of Managers, paid for sundry parts
1874 Dec 1, FF4, Balance sheet, vendor
1874 Dec 23, FF3, warden's letter, Warden
1874 Dec 23, FF3, Convicts received at the Colorado State Penitentiary from 13 June 1871 to 1 Dec 1874, Warden
1874 July 21, FF3, Cash Accounts of the Colorado Penitentiary
1874 Sept 30, FF3, Cash Accounts of the Colorado Penitentiary
1875 Aug 31, FF4, Balance Sheet, vendor
1875 Dec 6, FF4, Schedule of Vouchers Drawn, vendor
1875 Dec 7, FF4, Minutes of the Board of Managers, Warden (resigned)

1875 Dec 7, FF4, Minutes of the Board of Managers, vendor
1875 Jan 1, FF4, Bill for G W Graham, warden
1875 June 4, FF4, Minutes of the Board of Managers, vendor
1875 Mar 1, FF4, Minutes of the Board of Managers, expenditures
1875 Mar 3, FF4, Minutes of the Board of Managers, officer
1875 Sept 2, FF4, Minutes of the Board of Managers, vendor

Prosser, Warden
1874 Dec 31, FF4, Expenses paid for G W Graham & Switterline, US Prisoners, Warden

Pryce, Theodore
1874 Dec 1, FF3, Convicts in Colorado Penitentiary on 1 Dec 1874, prisoner, Crime: murder, County: Fremont, Sentence: life, Age: 28, Occupation: stock raiser, 5 ' 8"
1874 Dec 23, FF3, Convicts received at the Colorado State Penitentiary from 13 June 1871 to 1 Dec 1874, Prisoner no. 85, Crime: larceny, County: Fremont, Sentence: life, Age: 28, Occupation: stock raiser, 5 ' 8", Complexion: dark, Hair: dark, Eyes: blue, Nativity: England, Education: reads and writes

Q

Quarry
1874 Aug, FF3, Table showing days worked, 59
1874 July, FF3, Table showing days worked, 33
1874 June, FF3, Table showing days worked, 16
1874 May, FF3, Convict Labor Administered by Anson Rudd, 8 1/2 days
1874 Nov, FF3, Table showing days worked, 5
1874 Oct, FF3, Table showing days worked, 83.5

1874 Sept, FF3, Table showing days worked, 20

Quinn & Platt
1875 Aug 31, FF4, Balance Sheet, vendor

R

Ramsford, Chas
1874 Dec 1, FF3, Convicts Escaped since Organization of the Prison, escapee no. 19, Crime: larceny, County: Arapahoe, Sentence: 1 yr, Age: 20, received 1874 Aug 27, escaped 1874 Sept 10, recaptured same day
1874 Dec 1, FF3, Convicts in Colorado Penitentiary on 1 Dec 1874, prisoner, Crime: larceny, County: Arapahoe, Sentence: 1 yr, Age: 20, Occupation: laborer, 5 ' 9 1/4"
1874 Dec 23, FF3, Convicts received at the Colorado State Penitentiary from 13 June 1871 to 1 Dec 1874, Prisoner no. 96, Crime: larceny, County: Arapahoe, Sentence: 1 yr, Age: 20, Occupation: laborer, 5 ' 9 1/4", Complexion: dark, Hair: dark, Eyes: grey, Nativity: WI, Education: reads and writes

Randolph, A E
1874 July 21, FF3, Cash Accounts of the Colorado Penitentiary
1874 Nov, FF3, Expenditures and Earnings of the Colorado Penitentiary, repairing arms

Ravcil, Jose R
1874 Dec 23, FF3, Convicts received at the Colorado State Penitentiary from 13 June 1871 to 1 Dec 1874, Prisoner no. 19, Crime: assault with intent to rape, County: Arapahoe, Sentence: 5 yr, Age: 23, Occupation: laborer, 5 ' 10", Complexion: dark, Hair: black, Eyes: blue, Nativity: NM, Education: none

Raveil, Jose R
1874 Dec 1, FF3, Convicts in Colorado Penitentiary on 1 Dec 1874, prisoner, Crime: assault with intent to rape,

Colorado Territorial Penitentiary

County: Arapahoe, Sentence: 5 yr, Age: 23, Occupation: laborer, 5 ' 10"

Ready, C G
1875 Mar 1, FF4, Minutes of the Board of Managers, Guard
1875 Oct 14, FF4, Schedule of Vouchers Drawn, Guard

Ready, Chas G
1876 Apr 7, FF4, Balance sheet, vendor
1876 Dec 31, FF4, Report of the Treasurer, vendor

Reithman (J J Reitchman & Co)
1876 July 10, FF4, Balance sheet, vendor

Reithman, J J
1876 Dec 31, FF4, Report of the Treasurer, vendor
1876 Oct 13, FF4, Balance sheet, vendor

Reynolds (Bain & Reynolds)
1874 Nov, FF3, Expenditures and Earnings of the Colorado Penitentiary, convict labor
1874 Nov 13, FF3, Cash Accounts of the Colorado Penitentiary
1874 Oct, FF3, Expenditures and Earnings of the Colorado Penitentiary, setting pier

Rice, J B
1874 May 29, FF4, Statement of Accounts, clothing

Rice, John B
1874 Aug 31, FF4, Minutes of the Board of Managers, Board Member
1874 Dec 1, FF4, Minutes of the Board of Managers, Board Member
1875 Mar 1, FF4, Minutes of the Board of Managers, Board Member
1875 Mar 3, FF4, Minutes of the Board of Managers, Board Member
1875 Sept 2, FF4, Minutes of the Board of Managers, Board Member
1876 Dec 31, FF4, Report of the Treasurer, vendor
1876 Feb 17, FF4, Balance sheet, vendor

Rice, Mr
1875 Dec 7, FF4, Minutes of the Board of Managers, Board Member

1875 June 1, FF4, Minutes of the Board of Managers, Board Member
1875 June 4, FF4, Minutes of the Board of Managers, Board Member

Rice, P A
1874 May, FF3, Cash Accounts from the Books of A Rudd, potatoes

Richards & Co
1874 Aug 31, FF4, Minutes of the Board of Managers, vendor
1875 Dec 6, FF4, Schedule of Vouchers Drawn, vendor
1875 Dec 7, FF4, Minutes of the Board of Managers, vendor

Rickard, C C
1876 Dec 31, FF4, Report of the Treasurer, vendor
1876 Oct 13, FF4, Balance sheet, vendor
1877 Apr 11, FF4, Balance sheet, vendor
1877 Jan 1, FF4, Balance sheet, vendor

Ripley & Bro
1874 Nov, FF3, Expenditures and Earnings of the Colorado Penitentiary, advertising
1874 Nov 2, FF3, Cash accounts

Ripley (Henry Ripley & Bro)
1875 Mar 1, FF4, Minutes of the Board of Managers

Rivial, J R
1871 Dec, FF4, December Bill for Fees, prisoner
1871 Nov, FF4, November Bill for Fees, prisoner
1872 Apr, FF4, April Bill for Fees, prisoner
1872 Dec 31, FF4, Dec Bill for Fees, prisoner
1872 Jan, FF4, January Bill for Fees, prisoner
1872 July, FF4, July Bill for Fees, prisoner
1872 May, FF4, May Bill for Fees, prisoner
1872, Aug 31, FF4, Aug Bill for Fees, prisoner
1873 Apr 30, FF4, April Bill for Fees, prisoner
1873 Aug 31, FF4, Aug Bill for Fees, prisoner

Board of Managers Reports, 1871-1877

1873 July 31, FF4, July Bill for Fees, prisoner
1873 June 30, FF4, June Bill for Fees, prisoner
1873 May 31, FF4, May Bill for Fees, prisoner

Robinson
1875 Jan 1, FF4, Bill for G W Graham, expenses for recapture
1875 Jan 1, FF4, Bill for J W Switterline, expenses for recapture

Robinson (Thornton & Robinson)
1874 Dec 31, FF4, Expenses paid for G W Graham & Switterline, US Prisoners, recapturing Switterline
1874 Dec 31, FF4, Expenses paid for G W Graham & Switterline, US Prisoners, recapturing Graham
1874 July 24, FF3, Cash Accounts of the Colorado Penitentiary

Rockafellow & Co
1874 May, FF3, Cash Accounts from the Books of A Rudd
1874 May 29, FF4, Statement of Accounts, potatoes, clothing, lumber
1875 Mar 1, FF4, Minutes of the Board of Managers, rent & room

Rockafellow, B F
1875 Dec 6, FF4, Schedule of Vouchers Drawn, vendor
1875 Dec 7, FF4, Minutes of the Board of Managers, vendor
1876 Apr 7, FF4, Balance sheet, vendor
1876 Dec 31, FF4, Report of the Treasurer, vendor
1876 Oct 13, FF4, Balance sheet, vendor
1877 Apr 11, FF4, Balance sheet, vendor
1877 Jan 1, FF4, Balance sheet, vendor

Rockafellow, Frank
1876 Dec 31, FF4, Report of the Treasurer, vendor
1876 July 10, FF4, Balance sheet, vendor

Rockafellow, Geo
1874 Aug, FF3, Expenditures and Earnings of the Colorado Penitentiary, stone

1874 Dec 1, FF4, Balance sheet, vendor
1874 July, FF3, Expenditures and Earnings of the Colorado Penitentiary, stone
1876 Apr 7, FF4, Balance sheet, vendor
1876 Dec 31, FF4, Report of the Treasurer, vendor
1876 July 10, FF4, Balance sheet, vendor

Roff, Frank I
1874 Dec 1, FF4, Balance sheet, vendor

Rogers, John
1871 Dec, FF4, December Bill for Fees, prisoner
1871 July 9, FF3, Convicts dismissed from Colorado Penitentiary 13 June 1871 to 1 Dec 1874, prisoner, release no. 5, Crime: larceny, County: Arapahoe, Sentence: 1 yr, Age: 58, discharged 1872 Jan 1, no remarks
1871 Nov, FF4, November Bill for Fees, prisoner
1871 Oct, FF4, October Bill for Fees, prisoner
1871 Oct 1, FF4, September Bill for Fees, prisoner
1872 Jan, FF4, January Bill for Fees, prisoner
1874 Dec 23, FF3, Convicts received at the Colorado State Penitentiary from 13 June 1871 to 1 Dec 1874, Prisoner no. 5, Crime: larceny, County: Arapahoe, Sentence: 1 yr, Age: 58, Occupation: laborer, 5 ' 8", Complexion: dark, Hair: grey, Eyes: brown, Nativity: Isle of Man, Education: reads and writes

Rood, M L
1875 June 4, FF4, Minutes of the Board of Managers, vendor

Ross
1874 June, FF3, Cash Accounts from the Books of A Rudd, hunting escaped convicts

Ross, Paul
1874 May 29, FF4, Statement of Accounts

Ross, Peter
1871 Dec, FF4, December Bill for Fees, prisoner

Colorado Territorial Penitentiary

1871 Nov, FF4, November Bill for Fees, prisoner

1871 Nov 4, FF3, Convicts dismissed from Colorado Penitentiary 13 June 1871 to 1 Dec 1874, prisoner, release no. 18, Crime: larceny, County: Arapahoe, Sentence: 3 yr, Age: 38, discharged 1874 Oct 3, pardoned by Act Gov Jenkins

1872 Apr, FF4, April Bill for Fees, prisoner

1872 Dec 31, FF4, Dec Bill for Fees, prisoner

1872 Jan, FF4, January Bill for Fees, prisoner

1872 July, FF4, July Bill for Fees, prisoner

1872 May, FF4, May Bill for Fees, prisoner

1872, Aug 31, FF4, Aug Bill for Fees, prisoner

1873 Apr 30, FF4, April Bill for Fees, prisoner

1873 Aug 31, FF4, Aug Bill for Fees, prisoner

1873 July 31, FF4, July Bill for Fees, prisoner

1873 June 30, FF4, June Bill for Fees, prisoner

1873 May 31, FF4, May Bill for Fees, prisoner

1874 Dec 23, FF3, Convicts received at the Colorado State Penitentiary from 13 June 1871 to 1 Dec 1874, Prisoner no. 21, Crime: larceny, County: Arapahoe, Sentence: 3 yr, Age: 38, Occupation: laborer, 5 ' 4 3/4", Complexion: light, Hair: dk brown, Eyes: blue, Nativity: NY, Education: reads and writes

Rouse

1874 June, FF3, Cash Accounts from the Books of A Rudd, distributing circulars

Rowe & Walker

1874 Dec 1, FF4, Balance sheet, vendor

Ruble, Geo & Co

1876 Dec 31, FF4, Report of the Treasurer, vendor

1877 Jan 1, FF4, Balance sheet, vendor

Ruble (Lobenstein Ruble & Co)

1874 Dec 1, FF4, Minutes of the Board of Managers, leather & tools

1874 Dec 1, FF4, Balance sheet, vendor

1875 Dec 6, FF4, Schedule of Vouchers Drawn, vendor

1875 Dec 7, FF4, Minutes of the Board of Managers, vendor

1875 June 4, FF4, Minutes of the Board of Managers, vendor

1876 Apr 7, FF4, Balance sheet, vendor

1876 Dec 31, FF4, Report of the Treasurer, vendor

Ruble, Geo

1876 Dec 31, FF4, Report of the Treasurer, vendor

1876 July 10, FF4, Balance sheet, vendor

1876 Oct 13, FF4, Balance sheet, vendor

1877 Apr 11, FF4, Balance sheet, vendor

Ruble, George

1876 Dec 31, FF4, Report of the Treasurer, vendor

Rudd, A

1874 July, FF3, Table showing days worked, 2.5

1874 July, FF3, Expenditures and Earnings of the Colorado Penitentiary, 2 1/2 days labor

1874 June, FF3, Table showing days worked, 6 .5

1874 June, FF3, Cash Accounts from the Books of A Rudd, telegraphing

1874 May, FF3, Convict Labor Administered by Anson Rudd, 11 1/2 days

Rudd, Anson

1874 Dec 1, FF4, Balance sheet, Warden

1874 Mar 14, FF4, Letter to the Warden, Warden

1874 May, FF3, Convict Labor Administered by Anson Rudd, administrator of convict labor

1875 Aug 31, FF4, Balance Sheet, vendor

1875 Dec 6, FF4, Schedule of Open Accounts, vendor

Rudolph

1874 June, FF3, Cash Accounts from the Books of A Rudd, cartridges

Rudolph, A E
1874 Dec 1, FF4, Minutes of the Board of Managers, repairing arms
1877 Apr 11, FF4, Balance sheet, vendor

Rumbrugh, C H
1874 May 29, FF4, Statement of Accounts, wood

Ryan, John
1871 Dec, FF4, December Bill for Fees, prisoner
1871 Nov, FF4, November Bill for Fees, prisoner
1871 Nov 4, FF3, Convicts dismissed from Colorado Penitentiary 13 June 1871 to 1 Dec 1874, prisoner, release no. 17, Crime: larceny, County: Arapahoe, Sentence: 3 yr, Age: 21, discharged 1874 Oct 23, pardoned by Gov McCook
1872 Apr, FF4, April Bill for Fees, prisoner
1872 Dec 31, FF4, Dec Bill for Fees, prisoner
1872 Jan, FF4, January Bill for Fees, prisoner
1872 July, FF4, July Bill for Fees, prisoner
1872 May, FF4, May Bill for Fees, prisoner
1872, Aug 31, FF4, Aug Bill for Fees, prisoner
1873 Apr 30, FF4, April Bill for Fees, prisoner
1873 Aug 31, FF4, Aug Bill for Fees, prisoner
1873 July 31, FF4, July Bill for Fees, prisoner
1873 June 30, FF4, June Bill for Fees, prisoner
1873 May 31, FF4, May Bill for Fees, prisoner
1874 Dec 1, FF3, Convicts Escaped since Organization of the Prison, escapee no. 2, Crime: larceny, County: Arapahoe, Sentence: 1 yr, Age: 22, received 1871 July 9, escaped 1872 Dec 6, still at large
1874 Dec 1, FF3, Convicts Escaped since Organization of the Prison, escapee no. 4, Crime: larceny, County: Arapahoe, Sentence: 3 yr, Age: 21, received 1871 Nov 4, escaped 1874 May 26, recaptured 11 June 1874
1874 Dec 23, FF3, Convicts received at the Colorado State Penitentiary from 13 June 1871 to 1 Dec 1874, Prisoner no. 20, Crime: larceny, County: Arapahoe, Sentence: 3 yr, Age: 21, Occupation: laborer, 6' 1/4", Complexion: light, Hair: dk brown, Eyes: grey, Nativity: Canada, Education: reads and writes
1874 Dec 23, FF3, Convicts received at the Colorado State Penitentiary from 13 June 1871 to 1 Dec 1874, Prisoner no. 12, Crime: larceny, County: Arapahoe, Sentence: 1 yr, Age: 22, Occupation: laborer, 5 5 3/4", Complexion: light, Hair: light, Eyes: blue, Nativity: NY, Education: reads and writes

Ryan, Joseph
1871 Nov, FF4, November Bill for Fees, prisoner
1871 Oct, FF4, October Bill for Fees, prisoner
1871 Oct 1, FF4, September Bill for Fees, prisoner

S

Saeton & Morris
1875 Mar 1, FF4, Minutes of the Board of Managers, horse hire

Saeton, A
1876 Dec 31, FF4, Report of the Treasurer, vendor

Sanderson (Barlow, Sanderson & Co)
1874 May, FF3, Convict Labor Administered by Anson Rudd, 38 days

Sarton, A
1874 Dec 1, FF4, Minutes of the Board of Managers, drayage

Sartor & Co
1874 Nov 13, FF3, Cash Accounts of the Colorado Penitentiary
1874 Sept 18, FF3, Cash Accounts of the Colorado Penitentiary

Sartor & Morris
1874 Nov, FF3, Expenditures and Earnings of the Colorado Penitentiary, horse hire and draying

Colorado Territorial Penitentiary

Sartor, A
 1874 Dec 31, FF4, Expenses paid for G W Graham & Switterline, US Prisoners, team hire to Rosita
 1874 July 24, FF3, Cash Accounts of the Colorado Penitentiary
 1874 July 24, FF3, Cash Accounts of the Colorado Penitentiary
 1874 May, FF3, Convict Labor Administered by Anson Rudd, 4 days
 1874 May 29, FF4, Statement of Accounts, straw
 1874 Oct, FF3, Expenditures and Earnings of the Colorado Penitentiary, livery
 1874 Sept, FF3, Expenditures and Earnings of the Colorado Penitentiary, drayage
 1875 Jan 1, FF4, Bill for G W Graham, team hire
 1876 Oct 13, FF4, Balance sheet, vendor

Scidmore, G B
 1874 Oct, FF3, Table showing days worked, 7.5
 1874 Oct, FF3, Expenditures and Earnings of the Colorado Penitentiary, vegetables
 1874 Oct, FF3, Expenditures and Earnings of the Colorado Penitentiary, 7 1/2 days labor

Shaffenbug
 1874 Mar 14, FF4, Letter to the Warden, Marshal

Shaffenburg, M A
 1871 Dec, FF4, December Bill for Fees, US Marshal
 1871 Oct, FF4, October Bill for Fees, US Marshal
 1871 Oct 1, FF4, September Bill for Fees, US Marshal
 1872 Apr, FF4, April Bill for Fees, US Marshal
 1872 Dec 31, FF4, Dec Bill for Fees, US Marshal
 1872 Jan, FF4, January Bill for Fees, US Marshal
 1872 July, FF4, July Bill for Fees, US Marshal
 1872 May, FF4, May Bill for Fees, US Marshal
 1872, Aug 31, FF4, Aug Bill for Fees, US Marshal
 1873 Apr 30, FF4, April Bill for Fees, US Marshal
 1873 Aug 31, FF4, Aug Bill for Fees, US Marshal
 1873 July 31, FF4, July Bill for Fees, US Marshal
 1873 June 30, FF4, June Bill for Fees, US Marshal
 1873 May 31, FF4, May Bill for Fees, US Marshal

Shaffenburg, Marc A
 1871 Dec 2, FF4, Auditor's Letter, US Marshal
 1871 Dec 31, FF4, Auditor's Letter, US Marshal
 1871 Nov, FF4, November Bill for Fees, US Marshal
 1871 Nov 7, FF4, Auditor's Letter, US Marshal
 1871 Oct 5, FF4, Auditor's Letter, US Marshal
 1872 Jan, FF4, January Bill for Fees, US Marshal

Sheetz, M M
 1874 July 17, FF3, Cash Accounts of the Colorado Penitentiary
 1874 Nov 13, FF3, Cash Accounts of the Colorado Penitentiary

Sheetz, Mrs
 1874 June, FF3, Cash Accounts from the Books of A Rudd, washing

Sheetz, Mrs M M
 1874 Aug, FF3, Table showing days worked, 7
 1874 Aug, FF3, Expenditures and Earnings of the Colorado Penitentiary, 7 days labor
 1874 June, FF3, Expenditures and Earnings of the Colorado Penitentiary, washing
 1874 Sept, FF3, Expenditures and Earnings of the Colorado Penitentiary, 1 day labor
 1874 Sept, FF3, Table showing days worked, 1

Board of Managers Reports, 1871-1877

Shepherd
  1874 Sept 14, FF3, Cash Accounts of the Colorado Penitentiary

Shepherd & Co
  1874 Aug, FF3, Table showing days worked, 13
  1874 July, FF3, Table showing days worked, 7
  1874 May, FF3, Cash Accounts from the Books of A Rudd
  1874 May 29, FF4, Statement of Accounts, coal & blacksmithing
  1874 Nov, FF3, Table showing days worked, 7.5
  1874 Oct, FF3, Expenditures and Earnings of the Colorado Penitentiary, 8 days labor
  1874 Oct, FF3, Table showing days worked, 11
  1874 Oct, FF3, Expenditures and Earnings of the Colorado Penitentiary, covering dash
  1874 Sept, FF3, Expenditures and Earnings of the Colorado Penitentiary, rep dash
  1874 Sept, FF3, Table showing days worked, 1

Shepherd (Wm Shepherd & Co)
  1874 Dec 1, FF4, Balance sheet, vendor

Shepherd, Sam
  1874 Oct, FF3, Expenditures and Earnings of the Colorado Penitentiary, wood

Shepherd, Samuel
  1874 Dec 1, FF4, Minutes of the Board of Managers, wood

Shepherd, Wm
  1874 Aug, FF3, Expenditures and Earnings of the Colorado Penitentiary, painting sign
  1874 July, FF3, Expenditures and Earnings of the Colorado Penitentiary, 7 days labor
  1875 Dec 6, FF4, Schedule of Open Accounts, vendor
  1875 Mar 3, FF4, Minutes of the Board of Managers, officer

Shepler, John
  1871 June 13, FF3, Convicts dismissed from Colorado Penitentiary 13 June 1871 to 1 Dec 1874, prisoner, release no. 1, Crime: larceny, County: Gilpin, Sentence: 1 yr, Age: 24, discharged 1871 Nov 26, sentence expired
  1871 Oct, FF4, October Bill for Fees, prisoner
  1871 Oct 1, FF4, September Bill for Fees, prisoner from Gilpin Cty
  1874 Dec 23, FF3, Convicts received at the Colorado State Penitentiary from 13 June 1871 to 1 Dec 1874, Prisoner no. 1, Crime: larceny, County: Gilpin, Sentence: 1 yr, Age: 24, Occupation: cutler, 5'7", Complexion: light, Hair: lt brown, Eyes: blue, Nativity: Germany, Education: reads and writes

Sherman, M O
  1875 Mar 1, FF4, Minutes of the Board of Managers, Guard

Shoe Shop
  1874 Nov, FF3, Table showing days worked, 25.5
  1874 Oct, FF3, Table showing days worked, 43
  1874 Sept, FF3, Table showing days worked, 19

Sill, F
  1874 Dec 1, FF4, Minutes of the Board of Managers, wood
  1874 July, FF3, Expenditures and Earnings of the Colorado Penitentiary, stone
  1874 July 12, FF3, Cash Accounts of the Colorado Penitentiary

Sill, Frank
  1875 Aug 31, FF4, Balance Sheet, vendor
  1875 Dec 6, FF4, Schedule of Open Accounts, vendor

Simms, A C
  1871 Oct 1, FF4, September Bill for Fees, prisoner
  1872 Apr, FF4, April Bill for Fees, prisoner
  1872 Dec 31, FF4, Dec Bill for Fees, prisoner

Colorado Territorial Penitentiary

1872 Jan, FF4, January Bill for Fees, prisoner
1872 July, FF4, July Bill for Fees, prisoner
1872, Aug 31, FF4, Aug Bill for Fees, prisoner
1873 Apr 30, FF4, April Bill for Fees, prisoner
1873 May 31, FF4, May Bill for Fees, prisoner
1874 Dec 23, FF3, Convicts received at the Colorado State Penitentiary from 13 June 1871 to 1 Dec 1874, Prisoner no. 7, Crime: larceny, County: Arapahoe, Sentence: 3 yr, Age: 28, Occupation: laborer, 5 ' 5", Complexion: colored, Hair: black, Eyes: brown, Nativity: DC, Education: reads and writes

Sims, A C
1871 July 9, FF3, Convicts dismissed from Colorado Penitentiary 13 June 1871 to 1 Dec 1874, prisoner, release no. 7, Crime: larceny, County: Arapahoe, Sentence: 3 yr, Age: 28, discharged 1873 May 18, no remarks
1871 Oct, FF4, October Bill for Fees, prisoner

Skidmon, G B
1875 Mar 1, FF4, Minutes of the Board of Managers, vegetables

Smith (Howe & Smith)
1876 Dec 31, FF4, Report of the Treasurer, vendor
1876 Oct 13, FF4, Balance sheet, vendor

Smith, D
1874 Dec 1, FF4, Minutes of the Board of Managers, venison
1874 Oct, FF3, Expenditures and Earnings of the Colorado Penitentiary, venison

Smith, E P
1874 Dec 31, FF4, Expenses paid for G W Graham & Switterline, US Prisoners, nurse at Rosita
1874 July 24, FF3, Cash Accounts of the Colorado Penitentiary
1875 Jan 1, FF4, Bill for G W Graham, nurse at Rosita

Smith, G N
1876 Dec 31, FF4, Report of the Treasurer, vendor

Smith, Geo N
1876 Oct 13, FF4, Balance sheet, vendor
1877 Apr 11, FF4, Balance sheet, vendor
1877 Jan 1, FF4, Balance sheet, vendor

Smith, John
1872 Apr, FF4, April Bill for Fees, prisoner
1872 Dec 31, FF4, Dec Bill for Fees, prisoner
1872 Jan, FF4, January Bill for Fees, prisoner
1872 Jan 3, FF3, Convicts dismissed from Colorado Penitentiary 13 June 1871 to 1 Dec 1874, prisoner, release no. 22, Crime: larceny, County: Weld, Sentence: 2 yr, Age: 19, discharged 1873 Aug 18, four months good time
1872 July, FF4, July Bill for Fees, prisoner
1872 May, FF4, May Bill for Fees, prisoner
1872, Aug 31, FF4, Aug Bill for Fees, prisoner
1873 Apr 30, FF4, April Bill for Fees, prisoner
1873 Aug 31, FF4, Aug Bill for Fees, prisoner
1873 July 31, FF4, July Bill for Fees, prisoner
1873 June 30, FF4, June Bill for Fees, prisoner
1873 May 31, FF4, May Bill for Fees, prisoner
1874 Dec 23, FF3, Convicts received at the Colorado State Penitentiary from 13 June 1871 to 1 Dec 1874, Prisoner no. 27, Crime: larceny, County: Weld, Sentence: 2 yr, Age: 19, Occupation: laborer, 5 ' 8 1/4", Complexion: light, Hair: lt brown, Eyes: blue, Nativity: OH, Education: reads only

Smith, Rev Geo N
1876 Dec 31, FF4, Report of the Treasurer, vendor

Soda Springs
1874 June, FF3, Cash Accounts from the Books of A Rudd

Board of Managers Reports, 1871-1877

1874 May, FF3, Convict Labor Administered by Anson Rudd, 7 days

Solander, Mary
1873 Apr 30, FF4, April Bill for Fees, prisoner
1873 Aug 31, FF4, Aug Bill for Fees, prisoner
1873 July 31, FF4, July Bill for Fees, prisoner
1873 June 30, FF4, June Bill for Fees, prisoner
1873 Mar 19, FF3, Convicts dismissed from Colorado Penitentiary 13 June 1871 to 1 Dec 1874, prisoner, release no. 50, Crime: manslaughter, County: Boulder, Sentence: 3 yr, Age: 42, discharged 1873 Aug 14, pardoned by

1873 May 31, FF4, May Bill for Fees, prisoner
1874 Dec 23, FF3, Convicts received at the Colorado State Penitentiary from 13 June 1871 to 1 Dec 1874, Prisoner no. 60, Crime: manslaughter, County: Boulder, Sentence: 3 yr, Age: 42, Occupation: abortionist, 5 ' 3", Complexion: light, Hair: light, Eyes: grey, Nativity: PA, Education: reads and writes

Solomon Bros
1876 Dec 31, FF4, Report of the Treasurer, vendor
1876 Oct 13, FF4, Balance sheet, vendor

Sonneberg, F
1872 Jan, FF4, January Bill for Fees, prisoner
1872 May, FF4, May Bill for Fees, prisoner

Sonneberg, Frank
1871 Dec, FF4, December Bill for Fees, prisoner
1871 July 9, FF3, Convicts dismissed from Colorado Penitentiary 13 June 1871 to 1 Dec 1874, prisoner, release no. 11, Crime: embezzlement, County: Arapahoe, Sentence: 2 yr, Age: 24, discharged 1873 Jan 1, no remarks 1871 Oct, FF4, October Bill for Fees, prisoner

1871 Nov, FF4, November Bill for Fees, prisoner
1871 Oct 1, FF4, September Bill for Fees, prisoner
1872 Apr, FF4, April Bill for Fees, prisoner
1872 Dec 31, FF4, Dec Bill for Fees, prisoner
1872 July, FF4, July Bill for Fees, prisoner
1872, Aug 31, FF4, Aug Bill for Fees, prisoner
1873 Apr 30, FF4, April Bill for Fees, prisoner
1873 May 31, FF4, May Bill for Fees, prisoner

Sonneberg, Fred
1874 Dec 23, FF3, Convicts received at the Colorado State Penitentiary from 13 June 1871 to 1 Dec 1874, Prisoner no. 11, Crime: embezzlement, County: Arapahoe, Sentence: 2 yr, Age: 24, Occupation: clerk, 5 ' 1 3/4", Complexion: light, Hair: brown, Eyes: grey, Nativity: Germany, Education: reads and writes

Sopris, Allen B
1874 Aug 31, FF4, Minutes of the Board of Managers, vendor

Stanley, O G
1874 Dec 1, FF4, Balance sheet, vendor

Steele, John S A
1874 Dec 1, FF3, Convicts in Colorado Penitentiary on 1 Dec 1874, prisoner, Crime: murder, County: Boulder, Sentence: life, Age: 31, Occupation: laborer, 5 ' 10"
1874 Dec 23, FF3, Convicts received at the Colorado State Penitentiary from 13 June 1871 to 1 Dec 1874, Prisoner no. 83, Crime: larceny, County: Boulder, Sentence: life, Age: 31, Occupation: laborer, 5 ' 10", Complexion: dark, Hair: dark, Eyes: grey, Nativity: NY, Education: reads and writes

Stone yard
1874 Nov, FF3, Table showing days worked, 6 0.5

49

Colorado Territorial Penitentiary

1874 Oct, FF3, Table showing days worked, 22

Suitterlin, Jno W
1874 Dec 1, FF3, Convicts Escaped since Organization of the Prison, escapee no. 14, Crime: misusing Post Office, County: Arapahoe, Sentence: 1 yr 6 mo, Age: 21, received 1873 Dec 3, escaped 1874 May 26, recaptured 11 June 1874
1874 Dec 1, FF3, Convicts in Colorado Penitentiary on 1 Dec 1874, prisoner, Crime: misusing Post Office, County: Arapahoe, Sentence: 1 yr 6 mo, Age: 21, Occupation: clerk, 5 ' 7 1/2"
1874 Dec 23, FF3, Convicts received at the Colorado State Penitentiary from 13 June 1871 to 1 Dec 1874, Prisoner no. 74, Crime: misusing Post Office, County: Arapahoe, Sentence: 1 yr 6 mo, Age: 21, Occupation: clerk, 5 ' 7 1/2", Complexion: fair, Hair: light, Eyes: blue, Nativity: IN, Education: reads and writes

Swartz, John
1874 Dec 1, FF3, Convicts in Colorado Penitentiary on 1 Dec 1874, prisoner, Crime: larceny, County: Gilpin, Sentence: 2 yr, Age: 31, Occupation: farmer, 5 ' 7"
1874 Dec 23, FF3, Convicts received at the Colorado State Penitentiary from 13 June 1871 to 1 Dec 1874, Prisoner no. 84, Crime: larceny, County: Gilpin, Sentence: 2 yr, Age: 31, Occupation: farmer, 5 ' 7", Complexion: light, Hair: brown, Eyes: hazel, Nativity: Germany, Education: reads and writes

Switterline
1874 Dec 31, FF4, Expenses paid for G W Graham & Switterline, US Prisoners, US Prisoner

Switterline, J W
1875 Jan 1, FF4, Bill for J W Switterline, escaped prisoner

Symes & Decker
1876 Dec 31, FF4, Report of the Treasurer, vendor

T

T C Saw Mill Co
1874 June, FF3, Expenditures and Earnings of the Colorado Penitentiary, lumber

Tailor shop
1874 Nov, FF3, Table showing days worked, 13
1874 Oct, FF3, Table showing days worked, 9

Talbot, C M
1875 Dec 7, FF4, Minutes of the Board of Managers, vendor

Talbot, C W
1875 Dec 6, FF4, Schedule of Vouchers Drawn, vendor
1876 Apr 7, FF4, Balance sheet, vendor
1876 Dec 31, FF4, Report of the Treasurer, vendor
1876 Feb 17, FF4, Balance sheet, vendor
1876 July 10, FF4, Balance sheet, vendor
1876 Oct 13, FF4, Balance sheet, vendor
1877 Apr 11, FF4, Balance sheet, vendor
1877 Jan 1, FF4, Balance sheet, vendor

Taylor, J W
1874 Dec 1, FF4, Minutes of the Board of Managers, venison
1874 Nov 16, FF3, Cash Accounts of the Colorado Penitentiary
1874 Oct, FF3, Expenditures and Earnings of the Colorado Penitentiary, venison

Taylor, Robert
1874 Dec 23, FF3, Convicts received at the Colorado State Penitentiary from 13 June 1871 to 1 Dec 1874, Prisoner no. 78, Crime: larceny, County: Arapahoe, Sentence: 1 yr, Age: 21, Occupation: laborer, 5 ' 6 1/2", Complexion: light, Hair: light, Eyes: grey, Nativity: PA, Education: reads only
1874 Mar 18, FF3, Convicts dismissed from Colorado Penitentiary 13 June 1871 to 1 Dec 1874, prisoner, release no. 57, Crime: larceny, County: Arapahoe, Sentence: 1 yr, Age: 21, discharged 1874 Oct 8, pardoned by Act Gov Jenkins

Board of Managers Reports, 1871-1877

Teich, Geo
1875 Dec 7, FF4, Minutes of the Board of Managers, vendor

Texas Creek I M Co
1874 Dec 1, FF4, Balance sheet, vendor

Texas Creek Saw Mill
1874 June, FF3, Cash Accounts from the Books of A Rudd

Thomas (Gano & Thomas)
1876 Dec 31, FF4, Report of the Treasurer, vendor
1877 Jan 1, FF4, Balance sheet, vendor

Thomas, Francis
1874 Dec 31, FF4, Expenses paid for G W Graham & Switterline, US Prisoners, nurse at Rosita
1874 July 24, FF3, Cash Accounts of the Colorado Penitentiary
1875 Jan 1, FF4, Bill for G W Graham, nurse at Rosita

Thompkins (Webb & Thompkins)
1876 Dec 31, FF4, Report of the Treasurer, vendor

Thompson, J B
1871 Oct 1, FF4, September Bill for Fees, Auditor
1871 Dec, FF4, December Bill for Fees, Auditor
1873 Apr 30, FF4, April Bill for Fees, Auditor

Thompson, James B
1871 Dec 2, FF4, Auditor's Letter, Commissioner
1871 Dec 31, FF4, Auditor's Letter, Commissioner
1871 Nov, FF4, November Bill for Fees, Auditor
1871 Nov 7, FF4, Auditor's Letter, Commissioner
1871 Oct, FF4, October Bill for Fees, Auditor
1871 Oct 1, FF4, September Bill for Fees, Auditor
1871 Oct 5, FF4, Auditor's Letter, Commissioner
1873 May 31, FF4, May Bill for Fees, Auditor

Thornton
1875 Jan 1, FF4, Bill for G W Graham, expenses for recapture
1875 Jan 1, FF4, Bill for J W Switterline, expenses for recapture

Thornton & Robinson
1874 Dec 31, FF4, Expenses paid for G W Graham & Switterline, US Prisoners, recapturing Graham
1874 Dec 31, FF4, Expenses paid for G W Graham & Switterline, US Prisoners, recapturing Switterline
1874 July 24, FF3, Cash Accounts of the Colorado Penitentiary

Thornton, Alex
1874 Aug 18, FF3, Cash Accounts of the Colorado Penitentiary

Thurmond
1874 Aug 26, FF3, Cash Accounts of the Colorado Penitentiary

Thurmond, V E
1874 May, FF3, Convict Labor Administered by Anson Rudd, 2 days

Tomkins (Webb & Tomkins)
1875 Dec 7, FF4, Minutes of the Board of Managers, vendor
1875 Mar 1, FF4, Minutes of the Board of Managers, hardware
1875 Mar 3, FF4, Minutes of the Board of Managers, hardware

Tompkins (Webb & Tompkins)
1874 Nov, FF3, Expenditures and Earnings of the Colorado Penitentiary, hardware
1875 Dec 6, FF4, Schedule of Vouchers Drawn, vendor

Tritch, Geo
1874 Aug, FF3, Expenditures and Earnings of the Colorado Penitentiary, hardware
1874 Aug 31, FF4, Minutes of the Board of Managers, vendor
1874 Dec 1, FF4, Minutes of the Board of Managers, hardware
1874 Dec 1, FF4, Balance sheet, vendor
1874 July, FF3, Expenditures and Earnings of the Colorado Penitentiary, hardware

Colorado Territorial Penitentiary

1874 June, FF3, Expenditures and Earnings of the Colorado Penitentiary, hardware
1874 Oct, FF3, Expenditures and Earnings of the Colorado Penitentiary, hardware
1874 Sept 10, FF3, Cash Accounts of the Colorado Penitentiary
1875 Dec 6, FF4, Schedule of Vouchers Drawn, vendor
1875 June 4, FF4, Minutes of the Board of Managers, vendor
1875 Mar 1, FF4, Minutes of the Board of Managers, hardware
1876 Apr 7, FF4, Balance sheet, vendor
1876 Dec 31, FF4, Report of the Treasurer, vendor
1876 July 10, FF4, Balance sheet, vendor
1876 Oct 13, FF4, Balance sheet, vendor
1877 Apr 11, FF4, Balance sheet, vendor
1877 Jan 1, FF4, Balance sheet, vendor

Tritch, George
1875 Mar 1, FF4, Minutes of the Board of Managers, hardware
1876 Dec 31, FF4, Report of the Treasurer, vendor

Turley, James
1872 Dec 16, FF3, Convicts dismissed from Colorado Penitentiary 13 June 1871 to 1 Dec 1874, prisoner, release no. 42, Crime: attempt to murder, County: Gilpin, Sentence: 1 yr 4 mo, Age: 42, discharged 1874 Apr 17, no remarks
1873 Apr 30, FF4, April Bill for Fees, prisoner
1873 Aug 31, FF4, Aug Bill for Fees, prisoner
1873 July 31, FF4, July Bill for Fees, prisoner
1873 June 30, FF4, June Bill for Fees, prisoner
1873 May 31, FF4, May Bill for Fees, prisoner
1874 Dec 23, FF3, Convicts received at the Colorado State Penitentiary from 13 June 1871 to 1 Dec 1874, Prisoner no. 51, Crime: assault with intent to murder, County: Gilpin, Sentence: 1 yr 8 mo, Age: 42, Occupation: machinist, 5' 7", Complexion: dark, Hair: black, Eyes: grey, Nativity: MO, Education: reads and writes

U

Unger, Charles
1872 Dec 31, FF4, Dec Bill for Fees, prisoner
1872 July, FF4, July Bill for Fees, prisoner
1873 Apr 30, FF4, April Bill for Fees, prisoner

Unger, Chas
1872 June 18, FF3, Convicts dismissed from Colorado Penitentiary 13 June 1871 to 1 Dec 1874, prisoner, release no. 33, Crime: larceny, County: Pueblo, Sentence: 1 yr, Age: 21, discharged 1873 Apr 15, no remarks
1874 Dec 23, FF3, Convicts received at the Colorado State Penitentiary from 13 June 1871 to 1 Dec 1874, Prisoner no. 41, Crime: larceny, County: Pueblo, Sentence: 1 yr, Age: 21, Occupation: laborer, 5' 9", Complexion: florid, Hair: very light, Eyes: grey, Nativity: PA, Education: reads and writes

V

Vaughn, H
1874 June, FF3, Cash Accounts from the Books of A Rudd, guarding

Voris, G M
1874 Dec 1, FF4, Minutes of the Board of Managers, potatoes

Voris, G W
1874 Oct, FF3, Expenditures and Earnings of the Colorado Penitentiary, potatoes
1874 Oct 24, FF3, Cash accounts

W

Walker (Rowe & Walker)
1874 Dec 1, FF4, Balance sheet, vendor

Wall, Chas
1875 Dec 6, FF4, Schedule of Vouchers Drawn, vendor

Board of Managers Reports, 1871-1877

1876 Feb 17, FF4, Balance sheet, vendor
Ward, Thomas
1877 Jan 1, FF4, Balance sheet, vendor
Ward, Thos
1876 Dec 31, FF4, Report of the Treasurer, vendor
Warner, M M
1876 Dec 31, FF4, Report of the Treasurer, vendor
1876 July 10, FF4, Balance sheet, vendor
1876 Oct 13, FF4, Balance sheet, vendor
1877 Apr 11, FF4, Balance sheet, vendor
1877 Jan 1, FF4, Balance sheet, vendor
Warner, Wm
1874 Dec 1, FF3, Convicts in Colorado Penitentiary on 1 Dec 1874, prisoner, Crime: burglary, County: Arapahoe, Sentence: 1 yr, Age: 29, Occupation: laborer, 5 ' 7 1/2"
1874 Dec 23, FF3, Convicts received at the Colorado State Penitentiary from 13 June 1871 to 1 Dec 1874, Prisoner no. 101, Crime: burglary, County: Arapahoe, Sentence: 1 yr, Age: 29, Occupation: laborer, 5 ' 7 1/2", Complexion: fair, Hair: dark, Eyes: blue, Nativity: OH, Education: reads and writes
Washburn, George
1874 Dec 1, FF3, Convicts Escaped since Organization of the Prison, escapee no. 17, Crime: larceny, County: Pueblo, Sentence: 1 yr 6 mo, Age: 24, received 1874 Apr 23, escaped 1874 July 22, still at large
1874 Dec 23, FF3, Convicts received at the Colorado State Penitentiary from 13 June 1871 to 1 Dec 1874, Prisoner no. 80, Crime: larceny, County: Pueblo, Sentence: 1 yr 6 mo, Age: 24, Occupation: bookkeeper, 5 '9", Complexion: light, Hair: dark, Eyes: blue, Nativity: PA, Education: reads and writes
Watkins (L A Watkins & Co)
1876 Dec 31, FF4, Report of the Treasurer, vendor

Watkins, L A
1877 Jan 1, FF4, Balance sheet, vendor
Webb & Thompkins
1876 Dec 31, FF4, Report of the Treasurer, vendor
Webb & Tomkins
1875 Dec 7, FF4, Minutes of the Board of Managers, vendor
1875 June 4, FF4, Minutes of the Board of Managers, vendor
1875 Mar 1, FF4, Minutes of the Board of Managers, hardware
1875 Mar 3, FF4, Minutes of the Board of Managers, hardware
1874 Nov, FF3, Expenditures and Earnings of the Colorado Penitentiary, hardware
1875 Dec 6, FF4, Schedule of Vouchers Drawn, vendor
Wells Fargo & Co
1875 Mar 1, FF4, Minutes of the Board of Managers, express
Wells, Charles
1872 Dec 31, FF4, Dec Bill for Fees, prisoner
1872, Aug 31, FF4, Aug Bill for Fees, prisoner
1873 Apr 30, FF4, April Bill for Fees, prisoner
1872 June 18, FF3, Convicts dismissed from Colorado Penitentiary 13 June 1871 to 1 Dec 1874, prisoner, release no. 35, Crime: forgery, County: Pueblo, Sentence: 3 yr, Age: 23, discharged 1873 Apr 18, pardoned by _____
1874 Dec 23, FF3, Convicts received at the Colorado State Penitentiary from 13 June 1871 to 1 Dec 1874, Prisoner no. 43, Crime: forgery, County: Pueblo, Sentence: 3 yr, Age: 23, Occupation: bookkeeper, 5 ' 4 1/4", Complexion: dark, Hair: black, Eyes: dk brown, Nativity: NY, Education: reads and writes
Wells, Luther
1877 Apr 11, FF4, Balance sheet, vendor

Welsky, William
  1873 Aug 31, FF4, Aug Bill for Fees, prisoner

Werkheiser (Allen & Werkheiser)
  1874 Aug, FF3, Expenditures and Earnings of the Colorado Penitentiary, hardware
  1874 June, FF3, Cash Accounts from the Books of A Rudd
  1874 May, FF3, Convict Labor Administered by Anson Rudd, 2 1/2 days
  1874 May, FF3, Cash Accounts from the Books of A Rudd
  1874 May 29, FF4, Statement of Accounts, hardware
  1874 Nov, FF3, Expenditures and Earnings of the Colorado Penitentiary, hardware

West, Geo
  1876 Dec 31, FF4, Report of the Treasurer, vendor
  1876 July 10, FF4, Balance sheet, vendor

Weston (Harper & Weston)
  1874 Nov 12, FF3, Cash Accounts of the Colorado Penitentiary
  1874 Sept, FF3, Expenditures and Earnings of the Colorado Penitentiary, stone

Wetherill, George R
  1872 Jan, FF4, January Bill for Fees, prisoner
  1872 July, FF4, July Bill for Fees, prisoner
  1872 May, FF4, May Bill for Fees, prisoner

White, E E
  1872 Dec 31, FF4, Dec Bill for Fees, prisoner
  1872 July, FF4, July Bill for Fees, prisoner
  1872, Aug 31, FF4, Aug Bill for Fees, prisoner
  1873 Apr 30, FF4, April Bill for Fees, prisoner
  1873 Aug 31, FF4, Aug Bill for Fees, prisoner
  1873 July 31, FF4, July Bill for Fees, prisoner
  1873 June 30, FF4, June Bill for Fees, prisoner
  1873 May 31, FF4, May Bill for Fees, prisoner

White, George
  1872 Apr, FF4, April Bill for Fees, prisoner
  1872 Dec 31, FF4, Dec Bill for Fees, prisoner
  1872 Feb 7, FF3, Convicts dismissed from Colorado Penitentiary 13 June 1871 to 1 Dec 1874, prisoner, release no. 26, Crime: larceny, County: Arapahoe, Sentence: 1 yr, Age: 23, discharged 1872 Dec 12, no remarks
  1872 July, FF4, July Bill for Fees, prisoner
  1872 May, FF4, May Bill for Fees, prisoner
  1872, Aug 31, FF4, Aug Bill for Fees, prisoner
  1874 Dec 23, FF3, Convicts received at the Colorado State Penitentiary from 13 June 1871 to 1 Dec 1874, Prisoner no. 32, Crime: larceny, County: Arapahoe, Sentence: 1 yr, Age: 23, Occupation: laborer, 5 ' 8", Complexion: dark, Hair: dk brown, Eyes: blue grey, Nativity: Philadelphia, Education: reads and writes

White, James
  1872 May, FF4, May Bill for Fees, prisoner

White, John
  1872 Apr, FF4, April Bill for Fees, prisoner
  1872 Dec 31, FF4, Dec Bill for Fees, prisoner
  1872 Jan, FF4, January Bill for Fees, prisoner
  1872 July, FF4, July Bill for Fees, prisoner
  1872, Aug 31, FF4, Aug Bill for Fees, prisoner
  1873 Apr 30, FF4, April Bill for Fees, prisoner
  1873 Aug 31, FF4, Aug Bill for Fees, prisoner
  1873 July 31, FF4, July Bill for Fees, prisoner
  1873 June 30, FF4, June Bill for Fees, prisoner
  1873 May 31, FF4, May Bill for Fees, prisoner
  1874 Dec 1, FF3, Convicts in Colorado Penitentiary on 1 Dec 1874, prisoner,

Board of Managers Reports, 1871-1877

Crime: robbery, County: Pueblo, Sentence: 4 yr, Age: 37, Occupation: machinist, 5 ' 11 1/2"

1874 Dec 23, FF3, Convicts received at the Colorado State Penitentiary from 13 June 1871 to 1 Dec 1874, Prisoner no. 26, Crime: robbery, County: Pueblo, Sentence: 4 yr, Age: 37, Occupation: machinist, 5 ' 11 1/2", Complexion: dark, Hair: dk brown, Eyes: grey, Nativity: OH, Education: reads and writes

Whitherell, Geo R

1874 Dec 1, FF3, Convicts in Colorado Penitentiary on 1 Dec 1874, prisoner, Crime: murder, County: Weld, Sentence: life, Age: 23, Occupation: laborer, 5 ' 8 1/3"

Whitman

1874 June, FF3, Cash Accounts from the Books of A Rudd, potatoes

Wight, Eugene E

1874 Dec 1, FF3, Convicts Escaped since Organization of the Prison, escapee no. 7, Crime: larceny, County: Arapahoe, Sentence: 5 yr, Age: 25, received 1872 June 11, escaped 1873 Sept 19, still at large

1874 Dec 23, FF3, Convicts received at the Colorado State Penitentiary from 13 June 1871 to 1 Dec 1874, Prisoner no. 40, Crime: larceny, County: Arapahoe, Sentence: 5 yr, Age: 25, Occupation: millright, 5 ' 11", Complexion: fair, Hair: lt brown, Eyes: blue grey, Nativity: VT, Education: reads and writes

Williams, G C

1874 Sept, FF3, Expenditures and Earnings of the Colorado Penitentiary, wood

1874 Sept 28, FF3, Cash Accounts of the Colorado Penitentiary

1875 Mar 1, FF4, Minutes of the Board of Managers, wood

Willis, Charles

1871 Dec, FF4, December Bill for Fees, prisoner

1872 Apr, FF4, April Bill for Fees, prisoner

1872 Dec 31, FF4, Dec Bill for Fees, prisoner

1872 Jan, FF4, January Bill for Fees, prisoner

1872 July, FF4, July Bill for Fees, prisoner

1872 May, FF4, May Bill for Fees, prisoner

1872, Aug 31, FF4, Aug Bill for Fees, prisoner

1873 Apr 30, FF4, April Bill for Fees, prisoner

1873 Aug 31, FF4, Aug Bill for Fees, prisoner

1873 July 31, FF4, July Bill for Fees, prisoner

1873 June 30, FF4, June Bill for Fees, prisoner

1873 May 31, FF4, May Bill for Fees, prisoner

1874 Dec 23, FF3, Convicts received at the Colorado State Penitentiary from 13 June 1871 to 1 Dec 1874, Prisoner no. 17, Crime: assault with intent to rape, County: Arapahoe, Sentence: 10 yr, Age: 23, Occupation: tinsmith, 5 ' 8 1/2", Complexion: light, Hair: dk brown, Eyes: blue, Nativity: MO, Education: reads and writes

Willis, Chas

1874 Dec 1, FF3, Convicts Escaped since Organization of the Prison, escapee no. 3, Crime: assault to rape, County: Arapahoe, Sentence: 10 yr, Age: 23, received 1871 Nov 4, escaped 1872 July 24, recaptured same day

1874 Dec 1, FF3, Convicts in Colorado Penitentiary on 1 Dec 1874, prisoner, Crime: assault with intent to rape, County: Arapahoe, Sentence: 10 yr, Age: 23, Occupation: tinsmith, 5 ' 8 1/2"

Wilsky, Wm

1873 Aug 19, FF3, Convicts dismissed from Colorado Penitentiary 13 June 1871 to 1 Dec 1874, prisoner, release no. 54, Crime: bigamy, County: Arapahoe, Sentence: 2 yr, Age: 41, discharged 1874 Jan 25, pardoned by ____

Colorado Territorial Penitentiary

1874 Dec 23, FF3, Convicts received at the Colorado State Penitentiary from 13 June 1871 to 1 Dec 1874, Prisoner no. 70, Crime: bigamy, County: Arapahoe, Sentence: 2 yr, Age: 41, Occupation: farmer, 5 ' 7 1/2", Complexion: light, Hair: light, Eyes: blue, Nativity: Prussia, Education: reads and writes

Wilson, J M
1874 Aug 7, FF3, Cash Accounts of the Colorado Penitentiary
1874 July, FF3, Expenditures and Earnings of the Colorado Penitentiary, stone

Wilson, James
1872 Apr, FF4, April Bill for Fees, prisoner
1872 Jan, FF4, January Bill for Fees, prisoner
1872 Jan 3, FF3, Convicts dismissed from Colorado Penitentiary 13 June 1871 to 1 Dec 1874, prisoner, release no. 21, Crime: murder, County: Pueblo, Sentence: 1 yr, Age: 24, discharged 1872 Nov 23, no remarks
1872 July, FF4, July Bill for Fees, prisoner
1872 May, FF4, May Bill for Fees, prisoner
1872, Aug 31, FF4, Aug Bill for Fees, prisoner
1874 Dec 23, FF3, Convicts received at the Colorado State Penitentiary from 13 June 1871 to 1 Dec 1874, Prisoner no. 25, Crime: murder, County: Pueblo, Sentence: 1 yr, Age: 24, Occupation: laborer, 5 ' 9 1/2", Complexion: dark, Hair: black, Eyes: brown, Nativity: OH, Education: reads and writes
1876 Apr 7, FF4, Balance sheet, vendor
1876 Dec 31, FF4, Report of the Treasurer, vendor

Witherell, Geo R
1874 Dec 1, FF3, Convicts Escaped since Organization of the Prison, escapee, escapee no., 5 , Crime: murder, County: Weld, Sentence: life, Age: 23, received 1872 Jan 3, escaped 1874 May 26, recaptured 10 June 1874
1874 Dec 23, FF3, Convicts received at the Colorado State Penitentiary from 13 June 1871 to 1 Dec 1874, Prisoner no. 29, Crime: murder, County: Weld, Sentence: life, Age: 23, Occupation: laborer, 5 ' 8 1/2", Complexion: florid, Hair: dk brown, Eyes: grey, Nativity: NY, Education: reads and writes

Witherell, George R
1872 Apr, FF4, April Bill for Fees, prisoner
1872 Dec 31, FF4, Dec Bill for Fees, prisoner
1872, Aug 31, FF4, Aug Bill for Fees, prisoner
1873 Apr 30, FF4, April Bill for Fees, prisoner
1873 Aug 31, FF4, Aug Bill for Fees, prisoner
1873 July 31, FF4, July Bill for Fees, prisoner
1873 June 30, FF4, June Bill for Fees, prisoner

Wolfil, D F
1871 July 9, FF3, Convicts dismissed from Colorado Penitentiary 13 June 1871 to 1 Dec 1874, prisoner, release no. 10, Crime: larceny, County: Arapahoe, Sentence: 3 yr, Age: 27, discharged 1874 June 15, no remarks

Wolfil, D Fred
1874 Dec 1, FF3, Convicts Escaped since Organization of the Prison, escapee no. 1, Crime: larceny, County: Arapahoe, Sentence: 3 yr, Age: 27, received 1871 July 9, escaped 1872 June 23, recaptured 25 June 1872
1874 Dec 23, FF3, Convicts received at the Colorado State Penitentiary from 13 June 1871 to 1 Dec 1874, Prisoner no. 10, Crime: larceny, County: Arapahoe, Sentence: 3 yr, Age: 27, Occupation: baker, 5 ' 6 3/4", Complexion: light, Hair: light, Eyes: blue, Nativity: Germany, Education: reads and writes

Wolfit, D F
1872 Jan, FF4, January Bill for Fees, prisoner
1872 May, FF4, May Bill for Fees, prisoner

Wolfit, D Fred
   1871 Dec, FF4, December Bill for Fees, prisoner
   1871 Nov, FF4, November Bill for Fees, prisoner
   1871 Oct, FF4, October Bill for Fees, prisoner
   1871 Oct 1, FF4, September Bill for Fees, prisoner
   1872 Dec 31, FF4, Dec Bill for Fees, prisoner
   1872 July, FF4, July Bill for Fees, prisoner
   1872, Aug 31, FF4, Aug Bill for Fees, prisoner
   1873 Apr 30, FF4, April Bill for Fees, prisoner
   1873 Aug 31, FF4, Aug Bill for Fees, prisoner
   1873 July 31, FF4, July Bill for Fees, prisoner
   1873 June 30, FF4, June Bill for Fees, prisoner
   1873 May 31, FF4, May Bill for Fees, prisoner

Wolfit, D T
   1872 Apr, FF4, April Bill for Fees, prisoner

Y

Yetter, Charles
   1873 Aug 31, FF4, Aug Bill for Fees, prisoner
   1873 July 31, FF4, July Bill for Fees, prisoner
   1873 June 30, FF4, June Bill for Fees, prisoner

Yetter, Chas
   1874 Dec 1, FF3, Convicts Escaped since Organization of the Prison, escapee no. 9, Crime: robbery, County: Jefferson, Sentence: 7 yr, Age: 29, received 1873 June 20, escaped 1874 May 26, recaptured 11 June 1874
   1874 Dec 1, FF3, Convicts in Colorado Penitentiary on 1 Dec 1874, prisoner, Crime: robbery, County: Jefferson, Sentence: 7 yr, Age: 21, Occupation: laborer, 5' 10 1/2"
   1874 Dec 23, FF3, Convicts received at the Colorado State Penitentiary from 13 June 1871 to 1 Dec 1874, Prisoner no. 63, Crime: robbery, County: Jefferson, Sentence: 7 yr, Age: 21, Occupation: laborer, 5' 10 1/2", Complexion: light, Hair: light, Eyes: blue, Nativity: IL, Education: reads and writes

Additional Colorado Research Titles

If you borrowed this copy from a library and would like to order a copy, please send a check or money order to: Iron Gate Publishing, P.O. Box 999, Niwot, CO 80544. Our research books are available online to institutions and individuals at Amazon.com and on our website:

www.irongate.com

Boulder County, Colorado School Census 1877: An Annotated Index
    ISBN 978-1-68224-035-9 $15.95 + $4.00 S&H

Boulder County, Colorado, District Court, Petit Jury Lists, 1883-1910: An Annotated Index
    ISBN 978-1-68224-034-2 $11.95 + $4.00 S&H

Boulder County, Colorado District Court, Petit Jury Records, 1867-1936: An Annotated Index
    ISBN 978-1-68224-031-1 $24.95 + $5.00 S&H

Boulder County, Colorado District Court, Grand Jury Records, 1867-1922: An Annotated Index
    ISBN 978-1-68224-032-8 $11.95 + $4.00 S&H

Boulder County, Colorado Surveys and Mineral Claims at the General Land Office, 1859-1876: An Annotated Index
    ISBN 978-1-68224-030-4 $15.95 + $4.00 S&H

Boulder County, Colorado Clerk & Recorder, Loose Papers Box 1, 1861-1878: An Annotated Index
    ISBN 978-1-68224-029-8 $21.95 + $5.00 S&H

Boulder County, Colorado Clerk & Recorder, Loose Papers Box 2, 1861-1878: An Annotated Index
    ISBN 978-1-68224-028-1 $21.95 + $5.00 S&H

Boulder County, Colorado District Court Judge's Docket, Vol 1, 1867-1871: An Annotated Index
    ISBN 978-1-68224-026-7 $15.95 + $4.00 S&H

Boulder County, Colorado District Court Record, June 1862 to March 1866: An Annotated Transcription
    ISBN 978-1-68224-024-3 $11.95 + $4.00 S&H

Boulder County, Colorado Treasurer, Register of Accounts, 1867-1880: An Annotated Index
    ISBN 978-1-68224-023-6 $19.95 + $5.00 S&H

Inventors in the Colorado Territory and their U.S. Patents, 1861-1876: An Annotated Index
ISBN 978-1-68224-022-9 $54.95 + $5.00 S&H

Boulder County, Colorado County Court Index Book I, Plaintiffs and Defendants: An Annotated Index
ISBN 978-1-68224-021-2 $34.95 + $5.00

Minutes of the Board of Trustees of the University of Colorado, 1870-1876: An Annotated Index
ISBN 978-1-68224-020-5 $11.95 + $4.00 S&H

Boulder County, Colorado District Court Civil Appearance Docket, 1878-1882: An Annotated Index
ISBN 978-1-68224-019-9 $19.95 + $5.00 S&H

Boulder County, Colorado County Court Will Record, Volume A, 1875-1889: An Annotated Index
ISBN 978-1-68224-018-2 $11.95 + $4.00 S&H

Boulder County, Colorado, County Court Probate Record, Vol 1, 1875-1884: An Annotated Index
ISBN 978-1-68224-017-5 $11.95 + $4.00 S&H

Early Land Owners Along the St. Vrain Creek, Colorado Territory, 1860-1861: An Annotated Index
ISBN 978-1-68224-006-9 $11.95 + $4.00 S&H

Boulder County, Colorado District Court Widow's Relinquishment, Volumes 1 & 2, 1889–1937: An Annotated Index
ISBN 978-1-68224-009-0 $11.95 + $4.00 S&H

Boulder County, Colorado, District Court Guardians Bonds, Vol. A, 1876-1902: An Annotated Index
ISBN 978-1-879579-78-1 $11.95 + $4.00 S&H

Boulder County, Colorado Probate Court Fee Book, 1874-1890: An Annotated Index
ISBN 978-1-879579-88-0 $11.95 + $4.00 S&H

Boulder City Town Company Lot Sales 1859-1864: An Annotated Map Guide
ISBN 978-1-879579-87-3 $15.95 + $5.00 S&H

Brainard's Hotel Register, Boulder, Colorado, 1880: An Annotated Index
ISBN 978-1-879579-86-6 $15.95 + $5.00 S&H

Boulder County Commissioner's Journal, 1861-1871: An Annotated Transcription
ISBN 978-1-879579-77-4 $45.99 + $5.00 S&H

Boulder County Commissioners Journal, 1871-1874: An Annotated Transcription
ISBN 978-1-879579-91-0 $39.95 + $5.00 S&H

Colorado's Territorial Masons: An Annotated Index of the Proceedings of the Grand Lodge of Colorado, 1861–1876
ISBN 978-1-879579-85-9 $29.95 + $5.00 S&H

Boulder, Colorado Teachers, 1878-1900: An Annotated Index
ISBN 978-1-879579-93-4 $11.95 + $4.00 S&H

Boulder County, Colorado District Court Execution Docket, 1875-1885: An Annotated Index
ISBN 978-1-879579-94-1 $11.95 + $4.00 S&H

Denver, Colorado Police Force Record, 1879-1903: An Annotated Index
ISBN 978-1-879579-81-1 $11.95 + $4.00 S&H

Boulder, Colorado Births 1892–1906: An Annotated Index
ISBN 978-1-879579-79-8 $11.95 + $4.00 S&H

Arapahoe County, Colorado Territory Criminal Court Index, 1862-1879: An Annotated Index
ISBN 978-1-879579-70-5 $11.95 + $4.00 S&H

Boulder County Probate Court Appraisement Record A, 1875-1888: An Annotated Index
ISBN 978-1-879579-72-9 $11.95 + $4.00 S&H

Boulder County Assessor's Tax List, 1875: An Annotated Index
ISBN 978-1-879579-55-2 $11.95 + $4.00 S&H

Boulder County Assessor's Tax List, 1876: An Annotated Index
ISBN 978-1-879579-56-9 $11.95 + $4.00 S&H

Boulder Valley Presbyterian Church Records, 1863-1900: An Annotated Index
ISBN 978-1-879579-58-3 $11.95 + $4.00 S&H

Boulder's Masonic Pioneers, 1867-1886: Members of Columbia Lodge No. 14, Boulder County, Colorado Territory
ISBN 978-1-879579-57-6 $15.95 + $4.00 S&H

Map: Boulder City Town Company 1859 Original Survey Map
ISBN 978-1-68224-000-7 $24.95 (PAPER) + $7.00 S&H
ISBN 978-1-68224-001-4 $74.95 (MYLAR) + $7.00 S&H

Map: Boulder City Town Company, 11 Aug 1859 Land Lottery Map Showing Lot Purchases
  ISBN 978-1-68224-002-1 $24.95 (PAPER) + $7.00 S&H
  ISBN 978-1-68224-003-8 $74.95 (MYLAR) + $7.00 S&H

Map: Boulder City Town Company 20 Sept 1859 Map Showing Stock Certificates Issued by Lot
  ISBN 978-1-68224-004-5 $24.95 (PAPER) + $7.00 S&H
  ISBN 978-1-68224-005-2 $74.95 (MYLAR) + $7.00 S&H

eBooks:
Make the Most of Your Genealogical Research Trip: Battle Plan—Washington, D.C.
  ISBN 978-1-68224-027-4 $5.95

Publishing Titles

If you would like to order one of these books, please send a check or money order to: Iron Gate Publishing, P.O. Box 999, Niwot, CO 80544. Our books are available online to institutions through Ingram, to individuals at Amazon.com and on our website:

www.irongate.com

Set Yourself Up to Self-Publish: A Genealogist's Guide
    ISBN 978-1-879579-99-6 $19.95 + $5.00 S&H

Set Yourself Up to Self-Publish: A Local Historian's Guide
    ISBN 978-1-879579-98-9 $19.95 + $5.00

Publish Your Genealogy: A Step-by-Step Guide for Preserving Your Research for the Next Generation
    ISBN 978-1-879579-62-0 $24.95 + $5.00 S&H

Publish Your Family History: A Step-by-Step Guide to Writing the Stories of Your Ancestors
    ISBN 978-1-879579-63-7 $24.95 + $5.00 S&H

Publish a Local History: A Step-by-Step Guide from Finding the Right Project to Finished Book
    ISBN 978-1-879579-64-4 $24.95 + $5.00 S&H

Publish a Memoir: A Step-by-Step Guide to Saving Your Memories for Future Generations
    ISBN 978-1-879579-65-1 $24.95 + $5.00 S&H

Publish a Biography: A Step-by-Step Guide to Capturing the Life and Times of an Ancestor or a Generation
    ISBN 978-1-879579-66-8 $24.95 + $5.00 S&H

Publish a Photo Book: A Step-by-Step Guide for Transforming Your Genealogical Research into a Stunning Family Heirloom
    ISBN 978-1-879579-67-5 $24.95 + $5.00 S&H

Publish a Source Index: A Step-by-Step Guide to Creating a Genealogically Useful Index, Abstract or Transcription
    ISBN 978-1-879579-68-2 $24.95 + $5.00 S&H

Publish Your Specialty: A Step-by-Step Guide for Imparting Your Research Expertise to Others
    ISBN 978-1-879579-76-7 $24.95 + $5.00 S&H

www.ingramcontent.com/pod-product-compliance
Lightning Source LLC
Chambersburg PA
CBHW061512040426
42450CB00008B/1581